Mari and Silke and the Honda just before we left Kansas City on our Western U.S. tour.

A German girl and an American girl meet through an exchange program in Germany in 1988. An unusual friendship develops that changes their lives forever. This true story is about destiny and learning languages. It's a story of close friendship, finding true love and looking for the best in other people—across cultures, across stereotypes and united by a love of good food.

This book is dedicated to the loves of our lives:

Dave Monnie and Doug Hahn

CROSSING BOUNDARIES

How One Semester Abroad Changed Lives

Enjoy the journey
Mari J Hahn
+
Silke Monnie

Silke Monnie

Mari J Hahn

Published by Alive and Well

ISBN: 978-0-9907447-2-6

Table of Contents

Illustrations by Silke Monnie

Chapter 1 *Mari, 1986*

Taking flight

Imagine a room full of eighteen- and nineteen-year olds, all adventurous enough to want to go on a study abroad program. They want to board an airplane and fly off to another country and live for five months away from their families. They want to speak a new language, learn another culture, go to class and live their daily lives in another place.

During my freshman year at Valparaiso University in Valparaiso, Indiana, my friend, Carol Jud, signed up to study abroad for her sophomore year. She asked me if I had any interest and invited me to one of the info sessions. I went. I looked at the other students gathered in the conference room in the Union. They were my age or a year older. There were more women than men. I recognized a couple of faces, but most of them were unfamiliar. Little did I know then, many of these people would become my travel companions, my roommates and fellow adventurers. Many had never been outside the United States. For some this meant their first airplane flight. But for all of us, this was our chance to step outside our comfort zone and cross boundaries—both physical and mental.

A sense of adventure permeated the room. I had never been outside the U.S., except to Canada. I had never had a passport. I sat next to Carol, listening to Hugh McGuigan, the Director of International Studies at Valparaiso University, discuss the various study abroad programs. The Cambridge, England, and the Reutlingen, Germany programs were actually mini-campuses of our university, complete with a Valparaiso University professor who moved to the country with their spouse and family for a two-year commitment to be the director of the satellite program. A big advantage for both of these programs? Classes were taught in English. That sounded good to me! I was a psychology major. I learned that all of the credits were designed to count towards a degree in the College of Arts and Sciences, so I'd still be able to graduate on time—a big selling point for when I had to bring it up with my parents for their permission and of course, funds.

Later that night, I called my parents. We had one phone attached to the wall in my dorm room. In 1986, cell phones were non-existent, and it was quite expensive to make long-distance calls, so I didn't talk with my folks often. I thought my parents would be supportive, but I knew they'd have a lot of questions about which country I would go to, the cost, how safe it was, and how well the program was run. We talked through the details that I'd gleaned at the info session. They agreed it sounded like a good program. They encouraged me to sign up. So, I paid my deposit for the Reutlingen, Germany program. I would go the spring of my sophomore year—1988. Carol Jud and another friend, Kris McLenahan, had signed up for the same semester. We were going to have a lot of fun.

Why Germany? The reason really begins with growing up as a Lutheran. Baptized Lutheran as a baby, church and Sunday School had been an integral part of my life ever since I could remember. My parents signed me up for Kindergarten at the Lutheran K-8 school that was a couple miles from our house. I grew up steeped in Lutheran faith and teachings about the early beginnings of the Lutheran church in Germany. Every October we celebrated The Reformation—the day in 1517 when Martin Luther nailed the 95 theses on the door of the Catholic church in Wittenberg, Germany. I participated in children's choir, singing *Stille Nacht (Silent Night* in German) every Christmas Eve, learning hymns by Luther, Bach, and Beethoven. I took pipe organ lessons and studied church music and learned many of the standard hymns by German composers. My high school required two years of a foreign language and although my mom wanted me to pick Spanish thinking it would be practical for the work environment, I chose German.

We would be the forty-first group of students to go to Reutlingen with the Valparaiso University study abroad program. I attended several sessions with the other students in "R-41" to prepare us for our semester. The sessions were led by the Director of International Studies and students who had studied in Reutlingen the previous year. They prepared us for some of the cultural differences and gave tips on how to cope in another country. They also shared practical details like how to exchange money, how to take the trains, how to keep in touch with our families while we were abroad, and where to find the good bakeries. These sessions gave me a chance to get to know the other seventeen students who would be going to Germany with me. It seemed like a fun group of people. There were four men and fourteen women. Many of them had German-sounding names and most of them had already studied a lot more German than I had. They had a wide variety of majors, mostly in the arts and sciences programs. Many were looking forward to the German beer and we were all old enough to drink it!

Chapter 2 *Mari, 1968-1980's*

Flashback

I am the first-born child of Alice and Bob Johnson. I was born in Kansas City, Missouri, in the Midwestern part of the United States during the All-Star baseball game in July, 1968. I grew up in a neighborhood of single-family homes which had been built in the early 1900s on tree-lined streets, with nicely landscaped yards, and lots of churches.

My brother, Dean, was born two years later, and we grew up playing kickball in the street and riding our bikes all around the neighborhood. Our backyard was a popular hangout for neighbor kids as we had a huge Sycamore shade tree, a tire swing and an oversized sandbox. My summer birthday included homemade ice cream churned in the big ice cream maker out in the backyard and my mom's chocolate Wacky Cake. My mom made amazing theme cakes for birthdays—frosted and decorated masterpieces like Raggedy Ann and train-shaped cakes.

My parents were both college graduates. My dad worked full time for the federal government and my mom worked part-time as a home economist. We had one of the first microwave ovens which she used for recipe testing for Amana—The Radar Range. She also worked for Rival and developed several early Crock Pot recipes.

My brother and I liked to collect baseball cards. We were Royals' fans. The George Brett card was by far the best card. Sometimes on summer weekends we went as a family to watch the Royals play which was quite a thrill for us kids.

When I was in second grade we got a puppy. Our dog was black with white legs, so we named her Pippi Longstockings. She was a great lap dog. She slept at the foot of my bed every night, and she traveled with us on many a camping trip or on road trips to visit my grand-parents. My dad's parents lived in Nebraska and my mom's parents lived on a farm in Iowa, and we visited them often on weekends.

My mom encouraged me to journal often. It became the best way I knew to process my feelings and jot down the important events. I have stacks of filled journals from my younger years. There was one special journal that I started at the age of eleven. My mom gave it to me for Christmas that year. Instead of being in chronological order, I used it as a "special occasion" journal. It had a blue denim pattern and two goofy little gnomes on the cover and right on the front it says Gnome Gnotebook.

My parents made family vacations a priority. We liked to camp. When I was little we camped in a big army green tent. As I got older, we bought a pop-up camper, which was much more comfortable and also provided more shelter from torrential downpours.

One day my dad was talking with my brother and me and he said, "How would you like to go on a big camping trip to Alaska?" Dean and I thought it was a great idea! And my mom went along with it. And so, in summer, 1981, we went on the trip of a lifetime. We planned for almost a year. We purchased the necessary gear. We bought a black full-size van and converted it to a camper, with a bed in the back, a large cooler and a portable potty. My dad arranged the time off work. We hitched up the pop-up camper to the converted van, loaded up the gear, the family and the dog, Pippi, and set off for Alaska.

In 1981, Alaska was more remote and less touristy than it is today. The gas stations were few and far between, so we had to plan the route carefully and make sure we had food and fuel enough to get to our next stop for the night. *The Milepost*—a thick paperback book outlining every mile of the Alaska-Canadian Highway—was essential, listing every gas station and campground along the route.

Alaska is beautiful: green and lush with mountains and rainforests. That trip was quite a bonding time for our family. We kept track of every wild animal we saw out the window—bald eagles, bighorn sheep, moose, and even bears! We spent hours in that van counting license plates from all over the U.S., quizzing each other on state and country capitals. A favorite pastime was listening to Kenny Rogers, The Oak Ridge Boys and Willie Nelson eight-track tapes. I was twelve and I taught myself to whistle during the long days in the van (for some reason my new skill was not always appreciated by my family members). Every few days we would make camp in a new campground—we each had our designated chores to set up, clean up, or cook the meals on the Coleman stove. Once camp was set up, my brother and I created fantasy lands, building structures out of tree branches and moss in the lush forest near our campsites.

We had very little communication with friends and family back home that summer as there was no internet nor smartphones and we were on the road—we couldn't even receive letters in the mail. Leaving all my friends behind for the whole summer was difficult for me. I cried the first several days of the trip. That trip taught me at an early age to plan what you can plan for and to expect the unexpected. It helped me learn to take educated risks, to appreciate cultural differences, and go with the flow. We tried new foods, made new friends and tried to experience the local culture.

As a teen, I hadn't figured out who I wanted to be in the world yet. I wrote pages and pages in my journals about my struggles trying to fit in. Friends let me down and I wrote about how it felt to be an outcast. I wanted to have friends who liked me just the way I was. I was very critical of myself and I took the slightest rejection very personally. I wrote about my faith and my struggle to find meaning in my life. I wrote about being rejected by a boy I liked. I switched schools between my second and third years of high school and made some new friends. My friend Annie introduced me to new music and new books I had not heard of before. I began to find my voice and start to identify my priorities in life. I wanted to go to college. I wanted to be more independent. My faith was important to me and I was starting to figure out what that meant. I wanted to travel and meet new people. I began to feel more confident as a young adult.

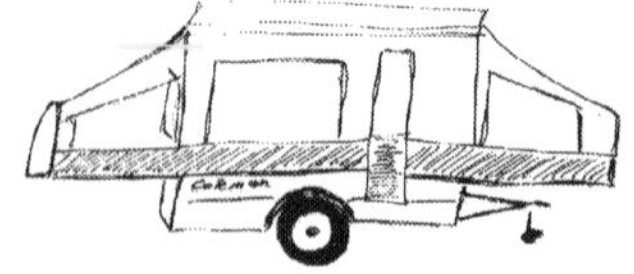

Chapter 3 *Silke, 1970's*

Growing up in Germany

I remember waking up as a child to bird songs too loud to ignore. Our house was just one block downhill from the forest in the little village of Staig in Upper Swabia in Southern Germany. The population in 1970 was about six hundred. It lay in a valley with the river Schussen running through it, surrounded by forests, other villages and farmland. We were able to walk to one little store that doubled as a bakery. You could see the Alps from our upper balcony.

My father was from Sudetenland (a German community for 200 years) in Czechoslovakia and in 1945, after the Second World War, he became a refugee and orphan at the age of nine because the Czech government expelled all Germans inside their country. He was raised by his older brother in Germany after they were forced out of Czechoslovakia. My father was first a mason and then became an architect. He designed and built our modern family home himself with help from my mother. Even though it was a more modern house compared to the other quaint old German farmhouses around us, my father took care to make sure it fit right in with the look of the village, adding a red clay tile roof just like the other houses. We had a huge yard with four apple trees in the center surrounded by fir trees.

As a small child I often woke up at night and climbed in bed with my mom and dad. They then made it very clear to me that I should stay in my own bed—so I climbed in bed with my older brother. He told me stories and sometimes got up with me in the early mornings in summer to take me up to the forest. We often sat behind a log and he would tell me to be very, very quiet. We saw deer, foxes, badgers and owls. I loved these times with him.

My mother would describe me as a wild child. It was hard for me to be indoors. She sewed me vinyl yellow overalls that she'd hose off with me in them before I was allowed to come back inside the house. I remember climbing into our apple trees in the spring, sitting very still, and absorbing the hum of the bees. My little sister, Selma, was my playmate if I wanted to play with dolls or Barbies, but if I wanted to play outside, I mostly played with the neighbor boys my age. Together we roamed the woods, built structures out of sticks, collected owl pellets, and dissected them.

We were not allowed to watch too much TV, but we could watch dubbed American shows like *The Waltons, The Brady Bunch, and Little House on the Prairie.*

Once I entered elementary school, I met a tomboy girl named Tine. The two of us were inseparable. Our favorite activities were long jumping into the manure pile in our underwear, mud fights in her parents' pond, and catching tadpoles. On the weekends we had campfires, watched the stars, and spent nights in the hayloft right above the sheep. We took the bus to the elementary school three miles away in a bigger village, and often Tine and I would skip the bus ride and run home down the hill—having mini-adventures, through fields and woods.

My mom was very religious and every Sunday my whole family went to church. In the southern part of Germany where we lived, most people, including my family, were Catholic. We helped my mom make lunch (which is the biggest meal of the day—usually some sort of meat with dumplings, gravy, and a salad). After lunch on Sundays, we strolled through the village or the woods. Sometimes my dad drove us to the lakes five miles from home. We swam, walked around the lake or walked barefoot through the swampy marsh trails. We all loved it and enjoyed each other's company.

After our little stroll, we'd have coffee and cake for the adults which often included my Tante (aunt) Johanna, and Onkel (uncle) Ventur, and herbal tea and cake or cookies for all of us children. My aunt often brought a cake as well. I love cakes—so Sundays were a very good day.

My mom or my older sister did all the cooking and baking on Sundays, and I took this job over after my sister moved out. Smells of lovage (a plant that looks and smells similar to celery and anise), pork roast and the sweet smell of a cake in the oven, filled the house. Eating healthy meals and drinking lots of herbal tea was very important to my mother. I learned a lot about cooking, collecting herbs in the woods, and sewing from her and at the all-girls Catholic school where we had cooking and sewing class once a week. It has been very beneficial in my life to have this knowledge. I am still learning more about herbal medicine and still love to cook and sew.

The only grandparent we had was my mother's mother, Anna. She lived in a small village bordering the Austrian alps. In her life, she had worked as a maid, a nanny, and in the local restaurants cooking for weddings into her eighties.

In her early thirties, Anna was raped by the farmer she worked for and gave birth to my mother. As a single woman in 1935, she was a disgrace in her village of Weiler im Allgäu, and so she left my mother, Mathilde, with her sister while she had to work. Her sister was married with two children and lived on a farm in Simmerberg. Johanna, the baby, was around the same age as my mother. My mom and her cousin, Johanna, grew up like siblings and we all called her Tante Johanna .

Needless to say, my mother and grandmother did not have a close relationship and my grandmother never forgave her for being born.

I, however, loved my grandmother. She was barely five foot one, but a very determined and strong woman who chopped her own firewood up until the day before she died in 1984.

My sister and I spent weeks of our summer or spring break in her apartment in the picturesque village, Simmerberg im Allgäu, in the mountains of Bavaria. She baked with us and made us amazing meals on her wood stove which was not only her heat source for her apartment, but also her only stove to cook and bake with. I remember one particular time my mom dropped us off. My mom told my grandma to make sure we ate our vegetables. As soon as my mom was gone my grandma asked us: "What do you guys want me to cook?" and our answer: "French fries and baked chicken." "And what would you like the next day?" We would say: "Baked chicken and french fries?"

So we skipped the vegetables and ate french fries and baked chicken all week, and we loved it.

Grandma Anna never learned how to drive so we took the bus to other villages to go grocery shopping or took cable cars up into the Alps to illegally pick Arnica flowers (it is a protected flower), which she made into a cream for aches and pains which she then gave to friends or kept for herself. The only toilet for the multi-unit building was down the hall, take a left, go down a dark, dank hallway to a tiny room with a pull chain toilet. I was scared to go there even in the daytime. Needless to say, we had a chamber pot at night under my grandma's bed. Selma and I loved it there. It was such a stark contrast to our modern family house. My grandma sewed us little white bonnets and we pretended to be Laura Ingalls from *Little House on the Prairie*. Often we played with children whose parents were on vacation in the little resort village.

When we cleaned out her apartment after she suddenly died of water retention (she was eighty) a month before my sixteenth birthday—I found my birthday gift, including a birthday card, in her closet… I will never forget that. It was hard for me to have her gone, and I felt upset that I hadn't had a chance to say goodbye to her and give her one more hug. A few nights after she died, I had a dream in which she went on a walk with me to visit many people that she said goodbye to. I did not know any of the people in the dream except my grandmother. At the end she said to me: "Silke, please know that I will always be with you. I can be closer to you when I am dead than if I were alive." Then she hugged me. I felt her cheek on mine when I woke up. I felt at peace.

While writing my final exams in high school I often smelled her perfume and it gave me comfort.

My mom's history made her a complex human being. She physically provided for us children but was not emotionally available. She did not really understand attachment to animals either, having grown up on a farm. I remember coming home from school when I was around nine years old and looking for my kitty. My mom told me that he was gone. I was very confused and asked her where he went. She told me that she had put him into a sack and had hit him with a hammer until he was dead. She was tired of taking care of him. This particularly hurt my relationship with my mother. I could no longer trust her. Shortly after that I realized that the rabbits that we would get in the spring, according to my mother, would keep on escaping in the fall out of the bunny hatch, and show up as "chicken" for a Sunday feast.

She kept geese every summer and Selma and I loved playing with the babies. One summer, however, the geese started honking at four a.m. every day. After a few days my mother had had enough. She said to me: "Silke, we are going to kill the one that is honking today. Come with me!" I said that I could not do that and Margot, my older sister, volunteered. I watched them. My mother herded the geese into the pen and then lifted them out one after the other, by their necks. She looked at them and asked: "Was it you?" One after the other, the geese just gave her a very scared look and didn't make a peep. She lost her patience and said: "If you guys won't tell me who the honker is, then you all have to go!" So, she killed them all.

My older sister and brother moved out when they were seventeen and eighteen. Now I was the oldest at home. It felt weird at first. The house was quieter, and Selma and I had to find our new positions within the family. Not long after that my father fainted (he was forty-five years old) in the bathroom and a bump as big as a fist protruded out of his chest. He had an aneurysm in the main aorta to the heart. They took him away in an ambulance and then in a helicopter to Tübingen, Germany, where there is a hospital that specializes in heart operations.

This started his slow decline and he was in and out of the hospital too many times to count. One year he was not home for Christmas, which made it even harder for all of us. Often, after operations, machines breathed for him, and a few times he started breathing on his own just before it was decided that the machines would be turned off. He needed another operation that was supposed to repair the arteries that go into his legs. He knew he needed to get another operation or die. The doctors tried to convince my parents to have the operation in the United States because it had been done there many times. No European hospital had ever performed this kind of procedure before. My parents would not consider going to the U.S. because they were afraid of the language barrier and not being able to understand the doctors. My father spoke a little English and my mom none at all. The University Clinic in Zürich, Switzerland said they would be willing to try it for the first time. My parents decided that a hospital that was two hours away from their hometown would be great. I am sure they had to sign a lot of paperwork so that my parents would not sue the hospital in case the operation did not work out, or he died. After the operation, the hospital staff thought that he was completely paralyzed and were not sure about his mental abilities.

When we got to the University Clinic in Zürich Switzerland, I went to his bedside. He opened his eyes and looked at me and said: "Spatzl (my nickname), beer." This told me two things. First, he knew who I was! Second, he wanted a beer! So, we went out and got him a beer and a straw. He drank the whole bottle. Over the weeks that he was in the hospital he slowly regained the movement of his head and arms but never his legs.

From one day to the next, our lives had changed completely—crossing from normal family life to living with a sick father who needed a lot of care. I feel like I lost my father that day. He used to be a confident, tall man who liked to crack jokes, but he transformed into a depressed, dependent, sad man.

When he finally returned home, my mom had rented a hospital bed and a Hoyer portable lift. The bed was in our dining room. Of course, there was a lot of sadness. My mom and dad cried often but we also had funny moments. One involved the Hoyer lift. My dad was a tall, heavy man and even though we were three people—my mom, Selma and I—we had a hard time lifting him. After we got the sling around his body, we tried to transfer him from his bed into the wheelchair. The whole device tipped over in slow motion. Thanks to all three of us being there, we slowly lowered him onto the ground. We all lay on the ground with him, just laughing our heads off. It was a ridiculous situation. One of us ran out and found a few strong neighbors to help us out and we put him back into his bed.

It was hard concentrating on school and my grades suffered. There was no psychologist helping our parents or Selma and I deal with this new situation, the sadness and our shifting responsibilities at home. My mom's time was occupied taking care of my father and we had to fend for ourselves. Often, I came home from school and cooked for everyone. I rode my bike to high school on bicycle trails through woods and farm fields to Ravensburg, about seven miles outside our village. To have this time to myself, rain or shine, was very helpful to me and cleared my mind.

Once I got stopped by a police officer on the bicycle trail in town because he saw that I had no reflectors. A few weeks prior, a new law had come into effect that all bicycles must have a front and back light, a repair kit and reflectors. He reprimanded me about my missing items and wrote me a ticket. That made me angry. I had no money. My parents would have to pay this bill. I don't know how, but I talked him out of writing me a ticket. I told him that a ticket was the last thing my parents needed right now and that it was really my safety issue.

There are so many rules in Germany that make no sense to me. Buckle up and get ready. You cannot mow your lawn, hang your laundry outside, do any kind of work that is visible to your neighbors on a Sunday (day of rest). Your garbage container has to be the same color as your neighbor's. In the south of Germany people clean their windows every Saturday and sweep their steps in front of their house (it is expected). I was really annoyed with all these rules. I sometimes felt that this country was not my country. I felt like I did not fit in.

We had to help out more around the house and in the care of my father. My older sister lived two hours away and could not come often. My brother helped out on the weekends with the projects around the house that required heavy lifting. I started mowing our property, helped my mom more around the house, and turned my father in bed so that he would not develop bed sores, which we had to deal with sometimes. They were as big and deep as a golf ball. Thank goodness he did not feel them. He had to deal with a lot of back pain though, and was on strong medications that we had to hide because my mom was worried that he would overdose. We also hid the knives—we were worried that he was suicidal.

My mom had to sleep with a buzzer—so that my dad could wake her up in the middle of the night when he was in a lot of pain and had to be turned in bed. My dad was limited to the entry level of our house and we had moved him from the dining room to his new room that was now in his former office. My mom slept upstairs in their bedroom. He later said, "If I had known I was going to end up in a wheelchair, I would have built our house without stairs."

In Europe you can go to the clubs (disco), when you are sixteen. Tine and I rode our bikes to Weingarten or Ravensburg—five to six miles away—and danced there but had to be home by midnight. The bus stopped running at nine p.m. I used to joke that our village rolled up their sidewalks as soon as nine p.m. struck. I felt so stuck there. I swore to myself that I would not raise my children in a country village. I would live in a city where you could go wherever you wanted, whenever you wanted.

On the way home from dancing, we took bicycle paths through the fields as fast as we could. Sometimes we were a little scared. Okay, maybe Tine wasn't scared, but I was. The thought that someone could be hiding in a cornfield and jump out at us was one of the fears in my mind.

I loved checking in on my dad when I got home. He usually did not sleep very much because he was in pain all the time. I would turn him in his bed and sit with him for a while, philosophizing about God and the world. One conversation really stuck out for me. He had ordered a book without my mom knowing. It was called: *Eunuchs for the Kingdom of Heaven.* It talked about the corrupt Catholic church and their priests. He let me read it when he was finished, and we discussed it. He tried to talk about newspaper articles or things that he had read with my mother but with her sixth-grade education, she felt threatened by intellectual conversations and got mad when she could not follow the flow of the interaction. He knew that I questioned the male Catholic institution and their exclusion of women. I had to keep going to church on Sundays and sometimes during the week in Catholic school to keep face for my family and our community until I moved out.

What I also learned during that time was that you know really quickly who your true family friends are. People stop coming by when tragedy hits you unless there is a true friendship. Thank goodness for my older brother and sister who came often to help and my Aunt Johanna and Uncle Ventur, who had his own metal shop. He built us a hoist that he attached to the ceiling in my dad's bedroom and in the downstairs bathroom to help get my dad in and out of the bed and the bathtub so he wouldn't end up on the floor again. We returned the Hoyer lift.

When I was thirteen years old, I had the same dream, three nights in a row. I was standing in front of a window with white and red checkered curtains. It was night time and I was looking at red blinking radio towers in the distance. I felt inner contentment and happiness. I was very puzzled by this dream.

My mom and dad were really busy with their own lives so there wasn't anyone to help me figure out what direction my life would take after high school.

In Germany, high school starts in fifth grade. In fourth grade we had to take a test in German, math, and general knowledge. The average of this grade determines which high school you will go to. The first one is called *Hauptschule*. This school will get you ready for blue collar work—butcher, baker, candlestick maker, mechanic, etc. After nine years of schooling, pupils apply to either companies or stores to start a three-year apprenticeship with a small stipend to work alongside experienced workers and learn a trade.

The second is called *Realschule*. This is where you go to learn about being an office worker, like a secretary, tax accountant, dental hygienist, etc. After ten years of schooling you can apply at companies to be an apprentice for two to three years.

The third is called *Gymnasium*. Schooling takes twelve years. This is the only high school diploma that allows you to apply to college or university. In Germany, schooling is paid for by the government. Depending on your grade point average, you can apply to certain universities. Schooling takes as long as it takes until you complete all of your credits for a certain degree, which means that some motivated people can get it done in three-to-four years. Others take five or more years.

I wanted to be a textile designer but in order to get into the program, I had to apply, take a test and wait a year. I wanted to move out and stand on my own two feet—be independent and not depend on money from my parents anymore. I felt bad leaving my family but knew that I was going to be only an hour away from them and would visit them often and help. I decided to first learn about how textiles are made and get my degree in Textile Technology/Textile Management. I thought it advantageous to know the process which would later help me get my foot in the door as a designer of textiles.

I applied for a student loan (University is free in Germany—students only have to pay for their living expenses. The student loan was just enough to live on). I was on my way to the Reutlingen University (*Hochschule Reutlingen*). Reutlingen University was well known in Germany for their textile education. My sister-in-law and I packed her car with my belongings and she drove me to Reutlingen, helped me settle in, then had to go back to her children at home. There I was all alone, in a strange city where I knew no one. There were no activities for freshmen students and no RA on our floor. I had to figure out my new life all by myself. I was scared and excited. I had waited for this moment for a long time. I wanted to be in control of my own life. I was ready to cross this boundary.

Chapter 4 *Mari, 1986*

College bound

In late summer, 1986, my parents and I filled our family van with my things and drove the nine hours from Kansas City, Missouri to Valparaiso, Indiana, to drop me off for my first year at Valparaiso University. There was the well-known flurry of activity that one might see on any university campus on move-in day. I was assigned to Lankenau 3 North. It was a hot day. We had to wait in a line for our turn with the elevator, to cram as much stuff on the elevator as we could to save ourselves from climbing up the three flights of stairs.

Lankenau was an all-girls dorm, with mostly freshmen. My roommate, whom I was meeting for the first time, was Kris Malburg. She was from a suburb of Chicago. We had very different taste. My bedding, for example, was white with a pretty pink flower print and I had two pink and white striped towels. Her comforter was a bold black and white pattern, with bright red sheets and she had a whole stack of bold red and white striped towels. She brought her stack of AC/DC records and a record player. I had my Chuck Mangione, jazz and some classical albums. We both were a bit out of our comfort zone.

We got our things all moved in and set up. Then came the goodbyes. I can clearly remember my dad with tears running down his cheeks as he drove away in the family van, the same one we had driven to Alaska—hugging his oldest child goodbye, dropping her off far from home.

I became close friends with several people on "3 North" as we called it. One friend was Kim, who lived right across the hall. She and I were both in the Valparaiso University marching band. I played the alto saxophone, she played the clarinet. Kim and I walked over to band practice together. The marching band was small, very social, and an all-around congenial group of music-loving, friendly folks.

It was at marching band, the first week of my freshman year, that I met Doug Hahn. He was a senior, so he thought he was pretty hot stuff. He was tall with thick, wavy dark blond hair. He lived in one of the coveted first floor dorm rooms with a private bathroom in Brandt Hall, just across the parking lot from my dorm. His roommate was Dana Radke. Dana and Doug were in the marching band, too. Since their room was at ground level, their windows opened right up to the students walking by on the sidewalk. Kim and I learned which window was theirs and we would knock on it as we walked by their dorm. They would open the window if they were home and we'd strike up a conversation.

Doug and Dana's dorm had planned an ice cream social for the upperclassmen to reconnect after summer break. Doug and Dana didn't think it would hurt to invite Kim and I—two friendly, freshmen girls from the nearby dorm. So we went to the event, all of us chatting and laughing together as we ate our bowls of ice cream topped with sprinkles and hot fudge sauce.

Doug and I discovered we had Psychology 101 together. It was a challenging class for me—my first semester of college level classes. For Doug, a senior triple major with Math/Computer Science and the Honors Program, Psych was the easiest class he could take to fulfill his social sciences requirement before graduation. For him, it was a blow-off class and he always picked things up quickly. I, on the other hand, had to really apply myself to my studies. He offered to tutor me before tests.

Doug, being three years older than I, and a senior, thought I was too young for him to date. Instead, we stayed up late talking into the night, solving world problems or discussing various controversial topics of the day. We did have one date, however. Doug invited me over for Chicken Parmesan. It was very unusual for us to cook in our dorms—nearly all meals were eaten in the dining hall. But most dorms had a small kitchenette where people could heat snacks in the microwave or cook a frozen pizza. Doug's dorm had a full kitchen, which was rarely in use, in the basement. I wanted to dress up and borrowed a short skirt from the girl across the hall for the occasion. It turned out the date wasn't romantic at all as the common kitchen area, normally completely unoccupied, was also being used by the talkative Don Meyer, another senior. Don dominated the conversation. Doug and I could barely get a word in edgewise. I think we both thought that weird date was the beginning and end of any possible romantic relationship.

Chapter 5 *Mari, Winter 1988*

The power of a home-cooked meal

I didn't date anyone seriously in high school or college. I *wanted* a boyfriend. In fact, I spent a lot of my time hanging out with guys. I seemed to be attracted to amazing, funny, cute guys—who were gay. Or, I would want more from a relationship with a guy friend than what they wanted. Then I took their rejection very personally. I based a lot of my self-worth on whether or not guys liked me. But, I was about to leave for my semester in Germany, so, at that point, I really didn't care about guys. I had travel and world adventure on my mind.

I finished my fall semester of sophomore year and went home to Kansas City for winter break. My high school friends threw a bon voyage party for me before I left for Germany. They arrived bearing journals as gifts. By the end of the evening I had received no less than five blank books. My mom encouraged me to stick them all in my suitcase as I packed my bags, wisely knowing I'd have a lot to write about, immersed in German culture, travel and new adventures. I laughed at her—I couldn't fill one journal per month! We argued back and forth about how many I should take. In the end, I just took one and stashed the others in my closet at home. Of course, I also took my worn Gnome Gnotebook—the journal I had kept since 1979. After eight years of entries, it was still only two-thirds full. I knew I would experience many significant events as I experienced another culture. "Everything always works out" became my motto, my version of, "It will be fine in the end." I was about to find out just how true that statement was.

January, 1988 had finally arrived. It was time for my study abroad semester in Germany!

Five months seemed like a long time—the longest I had ever been away from home. I was very reflective as I packed my bags and my passport. I wondered if I'd be homesick. I knew I would miss my dog, Pippi. She was older, and I worried she might not live until I returned home. I would miss my college friends and the familiar routine of life on campus. I was concerned I'd forget how to play the piano, so I took along piano music for a few of my favorite pieces—surely they'd have pianos in Germany. The most difficult thing would be saying goodbye to my mom and dad and my brother.

It was time to meet up with the other students going to Germany with R-41. Many of us flew from our hometowns where we'd spent winter break, to O'Hare airport where we all met up at the international terminal. We were nervous. We were hopeful. We were curious. Some cried. We were about to embark on the biggest adventure of our lives. Our flight on Icelandair connected in Reykjavik, Iceland, then on into Luxembourg. I remember the long overnight flight. The flight attendants served free drinks with those little airline bottles of alcohol. All of us were under twenty-one, so being offered a free cocktail was a new thing! Once we landed, we met the Valparaiso University Reutlingen Study Abroad Director for the first time. Herr Kumpf met our group at the airport with a shuttle bus. He talked to us as the shuttle made its way through the lush, green German countryside. He was very wise and helped us know what to expect once we arrived in Reutlingen. He had arranged for the shuttle bus to stop along the way at Frau Bimlich's, a German restaurant where we were served a traditional German meal—our first taste of real German food.

Finally, we arrived in Reutlingen and the shuttle bus drove through the city and up the hill to the college campus where we were dropped off with our luggage at our dorms. This campus had a much more modern, compact, steel and glass look than the spread-out brick buildings and park-like atmosphere of Valparaiso University. We knew ahead of time which dorm we were each assigned to. My roommate was another R-41 student—Liesl Schroer. We got on the elevator and remembered what Herr Kumpf had told us; that the ground floor in Germany is not the first floor.

All the dorms were co-ed with guys and girls on the same floor. There were no restrictions at all about who could be in your room. At Valparaiso, my all-girls dorm had strict rules about when guys were allowed. Our room in *Theodore Wurm Haus* had large windows that opened very differently from windows at home. They had a handle that turned, allowing them to open slightly from the top to let in a little bit of air. The handle could turn another way to swing the windows wide open. Many of the German students had theirs open—even in January! Our room had built-in desks in front of the windows and two beds built-in along each of the side walls. Our room also had a sink which was very convenient. We had brought our cassette tapes of our favorite music and the students before us had left behind a cassette player with the proper style of plug for the German outlet. It didn't take long to unpack as we each were only allowed to bring one large suitcase. Before long we were settled in and slept our first night in our new home.

I get my love of travel from my dad. A Korean war veteran, loving father, and a person of great integrity, he has imparted gentle wisdom to me about many situations in his eighty-five years. He loves a journey. He's curious and patient and has a sense of adventure—a good combination for travel. He's very grounded and deep down he values the unstructured education that travel provides. And it's from him that I boil down my own story into this phrase: When you approach a new life experience with a sense of curiosity and openness, looking for the best in other people, it can change the course of your life.

My dad has called me Monkey since I was a little girl. He gave me this letter in January, 1988 as I left for the airport.

Dear Monkey,

We are going to miss you a lot while you are in Germany. But we want you to have such a wonderful time. What an opportunity to visit other countries and to see how different but how very much people are alike the world over. Most would like only peace and love in their lives. I know you will be a good ambassador for the U.S.A. We will help the phone company out by being in frequent contact with you while you are in Germany. Have a good trip. We love you very much,

Mom and Dad

Many of the details of our semester abroad were taken care of for us by the Director of International Studies—the housing, our plane tickets, and travel documents. Also included in our study abroad fee were three guided group study trips, all led by Herr Kumpf, who was a knowledgeable tour guide. Lodging, transportation, and meals for the group trips were all planned ahead and paid for. Even our dorm rooms were already pre-stocked with many essential items that previous Valparaiso University students left behind for us such as bedding, hair dryers, and perhaps, if you were lucky as Liesl and I were, a radio/cassette player.

However, there was one thing that was totally new for me. At nineteen, this was my first experience where my meals were not provided for me.

When I was growing up, home-cooked meals were the norm. My mom took her role of family cook very seriously. Dinner was the time to gather around the table, talk through the day's events and enjoy a home-cooked meal together. Our favorite dinner was a cheesy baked sandwich we called Olga Sandwiches—named after my mom's boss at her first job as a home economist. My mom loved to try new recipes and she encouraged us to try new foods. She had attempted to teach me some basic cooking skills before I left home, but somehow her lessons didn't seem applicable at the time. I have major regrets about that.

At Valparaiso University, where I had already attended school for three semesters, we had a full-service cafeteria right in my dorm that served hot breakfast, lunch, and dinner every day. There were other cafeterias around campus, too, and our meal card was valid at every location for unlimited food, plus there was late-night delivery. If we wanted a pizza or a sandwich it would be delivered right to our dorm lobby up until midnight.

So there I was in a new country, in an unfamiliar dorm, surrounded by people I couldn't understand, with no mom to cook for me and no meal card to swipe.

A couple weeks went by and I hadn't eaten a hot meal, but I hadn't exactly been going hungry either. I had walked through the park into town several times to the German bakery, *Zotz*, for a thick slice of their specialty – a warm, crumbly piece of poppy seed kuchen they called *Mohnkuchen*. They also sold sandwiches on German hard rolls. I walked to the local *Prima* grocery store, bought some of the familiar foods I found there – cereal, oranges, and almonds – and ate cold food in my dorm room. After consuming entire kilo bags of oranges, that got pretty boring. There was one cafeteria for the school, but it only served lunch. It was on the other side of campus and we had to pay cash to eat there, so I only went there a couple of times the whole semester. I was getting enough food. It's just that I wanted so desperately to eat hot, home-cooked, German food.

Reutlingen was a medium-sized city with a traditional German pedestrian zone (*Fussgängerzone*) that was the gathering place. Cars were not allowed in the Fussgängerzone and I loved the concept of a shopping area just meant for walking. I spent my free time walking around Reutlingen, often walking to the fountain in the city center. I drew a map of my regular walk from campus. I took a shortcut down the hill, through the neighborhood with lovely homes and gardens, through the park, past the music hall and into downtown Reutlingen. It was about a twenty-minute walk. I had rarely walked anywhere back at home. My family had two cars and we drove almost everywhere. We had a carpool arranged to take us to school. I had never taken any public transportation. I had never even so much as walked to the grocery store! The way the cities are designed in Europe makes them very walkable. I enjoyed my walks in Reutlingen and I began to go regularly to the bakery, the pub, the department store, and the outdoor market (farmers market).

In the German dorms, each floor had its own large kitchen that was the gathering place, the social hub of the floor. I was surprised to find the German students, both men and women, all seemed to know how to cook meals for themselves. There was no microwave, there were no frozen dinners, and (gasp!), no pizza delivery. The students shopped at the local grocery store often, and they went to the butcher and bakery, too. They had real ingredients on hand and they used the provided pots and pans to prepare food for themselves each day. They often laid out a simple German breakfast or lunch of meats and cheeses, jams and breads, a freshly baked German pretzel or bread roll and perhaps a sliced tomato, on a cutting board. Sometimes they even lit a candle. Each meal was a ritual. The German students also made themselves tea each afternoon and sat down with a pastry or snack to relax after class. They took time to talk and discuss their classes or events of the day. The kitchen was definitely the place to be in the German way of life.

This aspect of German culture was very appealing to me, but those first few weeks in Reutlingen, it seemed so intimidating. This kitchen was my first experience hearing native German speakers just chatting conversationally. They spoke so fast that I struggled to even grasp what topic they were discussing – so those first few weeks I barely entered the kitchen at all.

Part of me wanted to go in and meet people but I felt very self-conscious. If I really wanted to experience German culture while I was there, I knew the kitchen would be the place to do it. I was terrified to introduce myself and actually meet the other students. I didn't know how to cook and that was embarrassing. They all seemed so capable, standing at the stove cooking gourmet meals. Plus, I didn't want to be "that American" who only knew English.

The study abroad program had made it clear – we didn't have to be fluent in German to participate. After all, our classes were taught in English. But what was becoming very clear was that I desperately wished I had taken more than only the minimum required two years of German in high school, which seemed like a lifetime ago.

After a few weeks I became more comfortable with hearing the German language. And my desire to experience German culture was strong. So one day I walked down the hall and peeked in the kitchen. Inside was a woman I had seen several times. There was something special about her. Have you ever spotted someone across a room and thought, "I could be friends with that person?"

Silke was petite, with a spiky, Euro hairstyle that stuck up on top. She dressed in colorful, unique clothing some of which she had sewn herself. She wasn't afraid to wear one-of-a-kind jeans that she had customized with brightly patterned patches. She had a contagious laugh and she smiled a lot. There was something about Silke's energy or perhaps a glimpse into her soul, that jumped out at me. But I was in another country with very poor mastery of the language—I was definitely out of my comfort zone. Our connection was stronger than either of us realized—it was like we were drawn to each other. That day when I saw her standing at the stove in the kitchen, I walked in and introduced myself in German. I said that my German wasn't very good, but she didn't seem to care. She just brushed it off and we laughed. I asked in German what she was cooking. It was *Spätzle*—traditional southern German noodles. I watched her cook and we laughed some more. She was easy to be around. She gladly demonstrated how she cooked the noodles. I used German as much as I could, learning new vocabulary words every day. And so, in the kitchen of the German dorm, an unlikely friendship began.

For the next several days I entered the kitchen whenever I saw Silke in there. She cooked herself meals every day. She had an easy, comfortable way of seasoning a dish with just the right blend of herbs and spices that were completely unfamiliar to my Midwestern American tastes. Silke could even make a simple green salad taste delicious! She blended oil and vinegar in the bowl, sprinkled in a generous amount of her salad herb blend from a jar in her cupboard, added the torn lettuce and tossed it all together. I watched her assemble her breakfast of bakery rolls with a few slices of unfamiliar meats and cheeses from the German deli. Presentation was very important, even for a casual meal eaten alone. She made it all look easy.

Whenever I went into the kitchen, I asked her to show me what she was making. I was an eager student, wanting to learn about German culture and what made German people tick. I was especially interested in the herb blends she added to almost everything she made. She was glad to tell me about them. We had to use the dictionary to look up some of the herbs and spices. I hadn't heard of *Herbes de Provence* before, a traditional blend of herbs from the southeast (Provence) region of France. It's a blend of thyme, marjoram, rosemary, oregano, savory and some versions contain generous amounts of lavender. I was intrigued by the concept of her jars of herbs already blended together to create a balanced flavor. Silke seemed to know which blend would complement the food best as she easily moved around the kitchen.

Silke made me feel welcome in the kitchen and introduced me to some of the other students. There were some very colorful personalities. Gilbert from Africa who spoke English as his first language. There was the large-boned Polish woman named Manuela who we stayed away from, mostly. Her hair was long and greasy, and she spoke in an abrupt manner that made her seem unfriendly. My next-door neighbor, Martin, was very stylish. He always had on expensive, name brand clothes. There was Herman—a lean, lanky blond boy with wire-rimmed glasses whom I had a crush on. Christina was sweet—she was very light-skinned with straight, shoulder-length, black hair. And friendly Frank—the tall, thin, dark-haired German boy with dark-framed glasses who made himself gourmet salads, and he had a car. As my German improved, I was more comfortable hanging out in there. The atmosphere in the kitchen was lively and someone always had music playing. Many familiar pop songs from the U.S. were popular in Germany at the time—*Red, Red Wine* by UB40 and INXS *Need You Tonight* were played daily in the kitchen. Silke's smile, her laughter and her friendship became an important part of my experience in Germany.

As I began to buy my own ingredients and cook some meals for myself, Silke offered me the use of some of the herb blends she kept in her cupboard. I was touched by the offer—the herb blends seemed to hold a magical, mysterious quality for me. As I began to sprinkle them on my own meals of pasta or chicken, I started to feel like a real cook! I didn't want to seem like a mooch, so in the spirit of sharing cultures, I made her an American meal of hamburgers and frozen french fries served with small cans of Diet Coke that were sold in the German grocery store. We began to appreciate each other's culture and our curiosity kept us wanting to learn more.

I wrote at a later time in my journal, *"If I've ever believed in reincarnation, it is now. Silke and I were sisters or best friends or lovers, or something very close."*

Chapter 6 *Silke, Spring 1988*

Meeting Mari: "Mad Libs"

Life at *Theodore Wurm Haus* was busy. It was one of three high-rise student dorms for the University in the city of Reutlingen, West Germany in the Swabian Alps, a region known for abundant fairy tale castles, caves, and cliffside scenery.

I distinctly remember 1988, spring semester. I was listening to Depeche Mode, The Cure, and Suzanne Vega, pining for my ten-year-older boyfriend, Rainer, who had just graduated and moved back to his roots in the North of Germany. I had not heard from him since. I watched him pull out of the train station a few weeks prior: *"Auf Wiedersehen, mein Schatz,"* (Goodbye, darling), I had said, and meant it.

The only mode of correspondence was letter writing, and the only phone on each hallway floor (one phone for more than seventeen people) of our student housing, only accepted incoming calls. But Rainer had not called or written since he had left. I had his mom's address but no phone number. I was a little depressed and disappointed but went on with my life.

My room was on the third floor with seventeen other students. We shared a large kitchen which had a big table and many windows and a balcony overlooking campus and the surrounding neighborhood. One of the rooms on our floor got two new American exchange students every six months. They did not hang out with any of us in the kitchen. They were loud, drank way too much, seemed really self-assured, and partied all the time. Their hairstyles were different from ours. It seemed most of them had blow-dried, puffy bangs and parted their hair to the left or right. People in Germany wore bangs, too, but they were cut uneven, almost jagged, and if you had bangs, your part was in the middle. You could spot the Americans right away with their colorful college logo shirts and tennis shoes.

When Mari arrived to our floor, I noticed her right away. She was quiet, timid, very soft spoken, yet had a positive, approachable energy about her. I had the urge to talk to her which was weird for me because I hated the English language. I'd studied it since the fifth grade but struggled with the spelling and had not had many experiences that allowed me to speak it. My English teacher would tell me to just sound it out, but it never sounded like anything! During high school there were many times when I would say to my father, "I will never use this illogical, stupid language in my whole life! Why do I have to study it?"

Why is English so hard?
We'll begin with a box, and plural is boxes,
But the plural of ox becomes oxen not oxes.
One fowl is a goose, but two are called geese,
Yet the plural of moose should never be meese.
You may find a lone mouse or a nest full of mice,
Yet the plural of house is houses, not hice.

Anonymous

Mari would only appear in the kitchen for short bursts, while it was the center of my social life. So, I had to be quick. I rehearsed what I would say in English in my head over and over. I surprised myself by my motivation and urge to say something in English and to actually talk to a native English speaker.

My parents were children during the second World War and learned how to survive on very little. They had sent me, the third child of four, to an all-girls Catholic school where home economics and cooking classes were part of the weekly curriculum. I loved to cook.

I was cooking my favorite dish, *"Käsespätzle"* (which is a version of homemade macaroni and cheese with caramelized onions and is a signature dish in the south of Germany), when Mari suddenly appeared in the kitchen. She was actually approaching me. I said in English, "Hi, my name is Silke," and reached out to shake her hand. She shyly took it and replied in German: *"Ich heisse, Mari. Mein deutsch is nicht gut."* (My name is Mari. My German is not very good.)

I said, *"Egal!"* and touched my hand to my lips and made a gesture by flicking my right hand over my shoulder, which young people did in Germany to say, "Whatever – it does not matter."

She was very interested in what I was cooking so I showed her how I made the dough for the noodles by putting flour into a bowl, followed by a pinch of salt and at least five eggs. I kneaded the dough very fast with a wooden spoon to make the dough airy and pushed it through the *spätzle* maker, which is a metal perforated grater with a square shaped cylinder that rides in the grooves and drips the dozens of perfectly formed noodles into the simmering hot water. Once they were cooked, I fished them out of the boiling hot water with a slotted spoon and transferred them into a big bowl. Grated cave-aged Gruyere cheese went in between each noodle layer, followed by a little salt and pepper. I let her make the next round of noodles and explained each step. It was a lot of fun showing her how to make one of my favorite meals. I delighted in her enjoyment of cooking and tasting this delicious dish.

We had an instant connection. I felt at ease and not self-conscious about my lacking English speaking skills. After my initial nervous attempts to converse with her, I became more comfortable and started to act things out. I doodled pictures on a piece of paper to make myself understood. I had also made sure that the German/English dictionary was not far from me. Mari had difficulties conversing as well but seemed equally motivated to communicate with me. I think what helped me feel so comfortable was that Mari had only had two years of high school German whereas I had studied English for eight years by then and even though my English sentence structure was not always correct, I could certainly make myself understood. It was also interesting how my brain would arrange the words in the right order after I had said it wrong. It is much easier to write in a foreign language because you have time to think about the word order. It is almost like your mouth is faster than your brain.

Cooking together became a regular practice. When words failed us, pointing, charades and general acting out worked well enough. Our little notes to each other looked more like *Mad Libs*. Instead of verbs and nouns there were pictures in place of our missing vocabulary. There was an instant connection and a mutual desire to spend time together.

Mari and I would sometimes walk through the hills from the student dorm and beautiful houses and gardens, to downtown Reutlingen to the Zotz bakery. When you opened the door at Zotz the smell of sugar, caramel and fresh baked pretzels and bread was heavenly. The staff was always happy to assist and we both enjoyed biting into the moist and flavorful *Kuchen*.

We often hung out with Frank who lived on our floor (I had a major crush on him). He was a very fun and funny guy and the three of us would go to town together to have a bite to eat or have coffee. We sat at local cafes and watched the people go by in the pedestrian-only zone as street musicians surrounded us with their beautiful music. I felt as if I had known Mari all my life. We had an instant ease and trust that was unexplainable. Being with Mari was comfortable from the start and I believe in my heart that we had known each other in a previous life. We just knew who each other was. There was no need to pretend. A magnetic pull brought us together. We both are adventurous, loving, food appreciators...creative people who are open to new experiences. But these things weren't clear when we were nineteen years old—we just knew.

I wanted her to meet my family and show her where I grew up. She was game and so we took the bus to my little village of Staig. My dad, Bruno had to either be in a wheelchair or laying in his hospital bed. My mom took care of him full-time and the German government paid her a salary every month.

My mom was overweight and had problems with her hips because of the daily lifting and care of my dad. My little petite sister, Selma, with her long brown straight hair was still living at home.

My family really liked Mari, especially when she played the piano in the living room. Her music filled the house and my dad seemed to forget all his burdens and would rock his head to the beat. In fact, he couldn't get enough of her playing so that when she ended one song he would say, *"Spiel mehr, bitte,"* (play more, please) and she would. When someone plays an instrument it is like a universal language where you articulate and evoke emotion.

That evening Mari and I helped my mom put together a simple German dinner of *Wurstsalat* (sausage salad). Mari and I were cutting the onions and lots of sausages while my mom made the dressing and cut some bread to go along with the sausage salad and of course *Hefeweizen (*German wheat beer*)*. My mom communicated by cooking, baking, and setting the table with a colorful tablecloth and flowers to show Mari that she was welcome. She wasn't able to speak one word of English. She'd been forced to quit her schooling to earn a living as a seamstress and worked in a sewing factory while my dad went to the university. She paid for their combined room and board while he finished his degree in architecture. My father would not have been able to finish school as fast as he did without her. He had no parents to help him out. He promised my mother that once he was done with his studies, they would get married and she would not have to work for money for the rest of her life. Years later when I cleaned out my parents' house after their deaths, I found a note from my father that he had given to my mother. It says: "Your truthful Bruno. I will always love you."

Selma's English was good enough to communicate with Mari, probably better than mine. She enjoyed day trips we took with Mari to the Lake of Constance (Bodensee – also called the Swabian ocean), where ferries took passengers across to other medieval towns on the opposite side of the lake to enjoy the view of the Alps and other sailing ships gliding through the blue water. On one of our outings we took her to the *"Affenberg"* (monkey hill) where nearly two-hundred macaques roam freely in a forest. You can even feed them popcorn! *Affenberg* is also home to a colony of white storks which you can experience in spring and summer. We loved going there and were really excited to show Mari. We all had a wonderful day walking on the wide paths that were lined with wooden horizontal poles that the monkeys could sit on and wait for people to offer some popcorn. It is a wonderful feeling to be so close to the monkeys and it tickles when their tiny little hands take the popcorn out of yours.

Back on campus, I turned twenty and we had a big party on a warm night in May. In the kitchen on the third floor, Mari and I cooked spaghetti and mixed a side salad for everyone on my floor. My friend, Tine, came and made my favorite cheesecake to share with everyone. I love creating community by sharing a meal with people. Cooking spaghetti might not sound very complicated but when you are cooking for seventeen people it helps a lot to have some extra hands. Mari made sure to keep the noodles stirred in the several large pots on one stove while I worked on the tomato sauce on the other. I used lots of garlic, onions and fresh herbs and, of course, my favorite *Herbes de Provence.* We had fun seeing if the noodles were done by flinging one or two on the kitchen counter to cool them off before making sure that they were al dente. I would take two spoons and dip the sampling spoon into the hot and divine smelling tomato sauce, drop the sauce from the sampling spoon into the tasting spoon and let Mari try it and see if the sauce was done. There was a lot of laughter and noodle swinging.

One of my fellow students had huge speakers that he hooked up in the kitchen and we were dancing and doing the limbo while drinking German beer. The windows may have been open as well...I recall students mingling out on the balcony. We were having a very good time when all of a sudden two police officers appeared in our kitchen and asked who was responsible for the party. I stepped forward and they handed me a ticket for 150 DM (*Deutsche Mark*—the currency before the Euro). Someone had called the police, probably a professor who lived close to campus. That was a lot of money for me but the police showed no mercy. The next day, I rode my bicycle to downtown Reutlingen to the police station and showed them my ticket, a copy of my rental agreement for my dorm room and utility costs. I got 400 DM from the government in student loans for living expenses and 200 DM alone went to my rent and utility costs. After listening to my sob story, they reduced the fine to 20 DM. I was so relieved and happy that I had made the effort to talk to them.

At the end of her semester abroad, and after my graduation, Mari's mom, Alice, and dad, Bob, came to visit and I enjoyed meeting them. Frank and I met Mari and her parents for a meal in downtown Reutlingen. They were so friendly and said to us, "If you ever want to come to the United States, you will always have a home in Kansas City." I said, "Thank you," but thought that that would never happen, because I had no desire to go the U.S. at all. Through the lens of European news, America looked to me like a nation of oil-hungry people who had a former movie star for a president, and thought their way of living was better than everyone else's in the world.

Chapter 7 *Mari, Spring 1988*

A language all our own

Silke and I developed a vocabulary that was familiar only to us. It's like when you have a toddler learning to talk, others cannot understand what the child is saying, but as their mother, you've heard those sounds, those "words" before, and you have an association. You know the context. Because of all the time you have spent together, you know exactly what they're saying. It must've been comical or impossible for another person to understand Silke and me. Mostly we spoke in German. I was, after all, living in Germany and trying to learn the language and culture. We used hand motions and would often grab a nearby pad of paper and sketch a simple drawing, Pictionary style, for an object we didn't know the word for. We relied on our German/English dictionaries. In addition, amazingly, I was becoming fluent in German! They say that once you start dreaming in another language, that indicates that you're comfortably fluent. I was definitely dreaming in German! We spent so much time together in the kitchen, we knew what each other meant to say, even if the grammar or the proper word didn't come easily to us.

However, we did speak a little bit in English. There was one phrase we came up with in English that we both understood—*"that is not the love,"* was a simple phrase that held a deeper meaning for us. We didn't have the vocabulary for in-depth discussions about hate, injustice, political tension, or misogyny in the world. At that time, everyone in Germany was keenly aware of the wall between East and West Germany. It had torn lives apart. The tensions between East and West were a regular topic in the news. When we spoke of the wall, *"that is not the love,"* helped us comprehend the vastness of the injustice that people experienced.

We sang songs together – I taught her a song in German that I had learned as a young child and it had hand motions. It's a song about the music man from *Schwabenland* (southern part of Germany), who played several different musical instruments. Each instrument had its own sound and hand motions. The song ends with one additional verse, where the radio clicks off and the song ends. And Silke taught me children's songs she knew in German. Our time together was infused with laughter. We loved to laugh at our mistakes.

The American students' schedule was completely separate from the German students. We had classes Monday through Thursday. On Thursdays we were dismissed at lunchtime, not due back to class until Monday morning. This allowed for plenty of time for travel. During my semester abroad, the American students traveled nearly every weekend around Germany and Europe. The most common way to travel was by train and the main luggage was a large backpack. I acquired a backpack in Augsburg, Germany at an outdoor gear store.

In late January, some of us purchased passes that were valid for one month of train travel throughout Germany. We went to Baden Baden, Hamburg, Augsburg, Munich, Düsseldorf, Trier, Stuttgart, Ulm, Heidelberg, Nürnberg, Karlsruhe, and Hintersee near Berchtesgaden. I fell in love with Germany—the historic villages, the cobblestone streets, the tidy storefronts, the pedestrian zones where people gathered for shopping and fresh markets. I loved the rich smells of German food wafting from the bars and restaurants. I loved stepping into the beautiful, inspiring cathedrals that were at the center of nearly every town and city. I appreciated the efficient German train system. They were always on time and I learned how to read the train schedules and calculate the best route to get almost anywhere.

In March and April, the eighteen study abroad students all received Eurail passes, which were unlimited train and ferry travel throughout all of Europe. We could now go anywhere! The Eurail pass was included in our study abroad fee. We all received them on the same day to use as transportation for the required group trip to Rome, Italy. Herr Kumpf, our Valparaiso University Study Abroad Director, did a great job of shepherding our group. He educated us and advised us, but he also realized that by then we were all very independent world travelers, and he respected that.

My favorite of the study trips was Berlin. We got to see firsthand the wall between West Germany and East Germany. Berlin was the city stuck in the middle—half of it was in the free "West" side and half was under Communist East German rule. As a group, we stayed in a hotel in West Berlin and spent most of our time there, exploring the world class museums and cosmopolitan city. We did go through Checkpoint Charlie and we spent one surreal day walking through East Berlin—with the armed soldiers on every street corner suspiciously watching every move from our group of young American college students.

East Berlin was dirty and gray, and many buildings damaged during the war decades earlier still stood in ruins. Only a handful of people were walking around—there were almost as many soldiers with their military style weapons as there were pedestrians. There were very few shops and it was difficult to even find a restaurant that was open for lunch. The contrast with West Berlin, just on the other side of that wall, was shocking. West Berlin was lively and entertaining. It was a bustling, big city with people, shops, restaurants, bars, and nightlife all around.

Armed with our Eurail passes, we wanted to see as much of the continent as we could. We poured over our worn copies of *Let's Go Europe!* We conversed with other travelers at youth hostels to find out what destinations they had enjoyed and why. We pulled out our folded paper maps. If we still didn't know where to go that weekend, we walked downtown to the department store, bought a *USA Today* newspaper, Europe edition (in English), and flipped over the front section of the paper. There, they printed a color-coded weather map of Europe. We studied the colors, looked at the yellow and orange color bands to see which cities had the warmest weather forecast for the coming weekend, then planned our trip accordingly.

At that time, each country in Europe had its own currency. There was no Euro. It was quite an ordeal to exchange our German Deutschmarks for the local currency in all of these countries we visited. There was no such thing as an ATM machine. This money exchange had to be done in person at either the train station or a bank. You didn't want to exchange more money than you needed, because then there'd be a hefty fee to exchange the remaining currency back into German Marks.

May, 1988 Exchange rates:

U.S. Dollars to German Marks = 1.6
U.S. Dollars to Austrian Schillings = 12.4
U.S. Dollars to Italian Lire = 1,245
U.S. Dollars to French Francs = 5.6
U.S. Dollars to Swiss Francs = 1.41

What adventures we had—crossing the boundaries of many countries. I went to England, France, Spain, Italy, Greece, Switzerland,

and Austria. We slept on trains, and at least one night in a train station. We slept on the deck of the ferry to Greece. We stayed at youth hostels or sometimes at a smaller, local *pension* (inn), that fit our student budget. I met up with my high school friend, Annie, in Nice, France where we stayed at a local hotel for about twenty-five U.S. dollars per night. I traveled to Paris to meet up with my college friend, Kim Roller, who was studying there. She showed me all around the city. I loved Sacré-Coeur—a huge, white, domed basilica where we listened to street musicians and got crepes from the food cart. Kim spoke French and she knew her way around and she was familiar with the Metro which made everything easier.

I found France to be very frustrating when I didn't have Kim or Annie as my tour guide. I learned a few French phrases, but for the most part, I couldn't communicate with the people. They had different holidays than in Germany. On holidays, every shop, grocery store, bank and restaurant were closed. Their time zones changed on a different schedule than in Germany. With no internet and the only news was a newspaper in French, it was challenging to find out this information ahead of time. I spent many hours in France just waiting for a bank to open. I was in Paris over Palm Sunday weekend. I researched what time the Palm Sunday service was at Notre-Dame Cathedral. I thought it would be really amazing to attend Palm Sunday worship there! Even though the service would be in French, I wanted to experience the music and the people in that beautiful cathedral. There was a sign posted about the service times and I made a note of the service I wanted to attend the next day. I arrived at that time, but not realizing they had turned their clocks forward the night before, I got there just as it was ending.

My favorite places were the cities in Germany, Austria and Switzerland, nestled in the beautiful Alps mountain range. Even just riding on the train through the Alps was so beautiful. I'd gaze out the train window, with my Walkman playing Mozart or Yes on my headphones.

When we traveled, our meals were usually simple—a trusty bag of almonds got me through many train rides. We ate at bakeries—baguette sandwiches layered with meats, cheeses and tomatoes. Sometimes we bought food at food carts. We saw the castles, museums and tourist sights. We walked miles and miles around cities throughout Europe. I filled my journal daily with stories, observations, details about new people, new places, new tastes and smells. We took photos (nothing was digital, so we couldn't see what the photos looked like until we returned to the States and got our film rolls developed). When I returned home that summer I had twelve rolls of undeveloped film. It was quite a treat to get those developed and relive the adventures!

Rome was another of our group study trips. This was the first city where I felt uncomfortable, even unsafe. Italian men would call out to us in English, "Hey, pretty lady, want to get married?" This really annoyed me. The gypsy children swarmed around us in the crowds of tourists near Vatican City, begging for money. That was startling. The cars and mopeds were fast and unpredictable, zipping around corners and nearly knocking me over. Herr Kumpf had advised us on how to be safe from the pickpockets. We all had our money and passports tucked safely away in special zipper pouches under our clothes. We saw all the major sites—Vatican City, St. Peter's Basilica, the Sistine Chapel, the Coliseum and the Roman Forum. I'm glad I saw those places, but I decided I didn't like Rome. In fact, I said I never wanted to go back there—ever.

Following our Rome group trip, we had a one-week spring break. Three other girls from my study program and I headed to Greece. We took the train to Brindisi and the ferry from Brindisi to Greece. First, we visited Athens. Then, we set off for a beach vacation. We ended up in Tolon—"a small town stretched along a beautiful sandy beach and full of particularly friendly locals," read the brochure. It was a charming beach town near Nafplion. We stayed at the Hotel Flisvos, the four of us negotiating for a large, dorm-style room with a balcony overlooking the water. It was right on the beach and had a Greek buffet restaurant. Since it was off-season, we had almost the whole hotel to ourselves. Directly across the street was a small, neighborhood grocery store. We thought we were really living the life! Our daily routine became sleeping in, walking across the street to the store, buying small cans of Diet Coke and strawberries, and a few other snacks, and spending our afternoons on the beach, swimming in the turquoise blue water. The water was perfectly clear, very salty and cold, but not too cold to take a swim in just our bikini bottoms. At the end of the lazy day we walked back to the hotel, sunburned and tired. We would shower and change clothes and eat at the hotel buffet—delicious moussaka and eggplant dishes. The hotel owners gave us all postcards of the hotel and told us to return someday for our honeymoons with our husbands. We thought that sounded a long way off!

At the end of the spring break, all eighteen American students in our group filtered their way back to Reutlingen. Some had gone to other parts of Italy or other Southern European destinations. We all had to be back on campus on the same day to start classes. It turned out, many of us had connections on the same night train returning from Milano back to Stuttgart. We all met up in the train station. We were shocked to find one of our fellow students, Matt, who had run out of money, was panhandling in the train station to get a few lire for some food for his return trip. We were a little short of cash ourselves, but we had plenty of food. We all pitched in to make sure Matt had food for the return trip. The train wasn't too crowded, which was a relief. Liesl, Karl, Matt, Holly and I, had a compartment to ourselves. Karl had brought a bottle of gin, which we passed around. We shared tidbits about our various travels, talked about religion and what the future might hold. We caught the train from Stuttgart to Horb, then Tübingen and finally back to Reutlingen. The whole trip took fifty-eight hours. We were exhausted when we finally arrived back at the Reutlingen train station. I was too tired to walk the thirty minutes from the train station, through town, up the hill, back to campus. From the train station pay phone I called the hall phone at my dorm. Christina answered. I explained (in German, of course), about our long journey and how tired we were. She put Frank on the phone. Before we knew it, Frank had arrived in his car to give us a ride back to *Theodore Wurm Haus.*

One day as I sat in German class, Herr Kumpf knocked on the door of the classroom and called me out of class. I was alarmed—this wasn't normal. I gathered up my books. As we were walking back to my dorm, he explained that he had had a call from my parents. My grandmother had passed away the day before. This was my mom's mother, Iona Carlson. I called her Grandma Ony. Herr Kumpf asked me about her. I told him she lived on a farm in Iowa (although she had been in a nursing home the past year). I recalled her big, eat-in kitchen where she spent much of her time baking pies or making big mid-day meals, such as chicken and dumplings, with corn and vegetables from the garden. I reminisced about the times I had spent as a child with her there at the farm. She would let me carry a bowl of kitchen scraps out to the yard for the farm cats. She had a stepstool in the kitchen and I stood on it to help her mix up a cake or splash in the big sink full of dishes. In winter, she'd heat blankets in the dryer for my brother and I to take up to our beds as we headed up the stairs to the cold, drafty bedroom of the farmhouse. Every fall during apple picking season my grandparents drove to our house in Kansas City for a visit. They liked to pick bushels of Jonathan apples from Stephenson's Apple Farm and it was quite a treat to eat dinner at the famous Stephenson's Old Apple Farm Restaurant after a day of apple-picking. Then we took the apples home and made baked apples, apple pies or apple dumplings.

Herr Kumpf listened patiently to my trip down memory lane as we walked across campus. No one expected that I would fly home for Grandma Ony's funeral. Back at my dorm, I just laid down on my bed and cried. It was difficult to process this when I was so far away from home. I wished I had a friend to talk to. I found Silke in her room studying. I told her about my grandma passing away. She listened. She told me her grandma had passed away three years earlier. It was good to connect with somebody who understood what I was going through.

I wished I could have taken a trip with Silke, but the class schedule for the German students was much more demanding and Silke had no extra money for travel. Her classes were five days a week and required much more studying. I traveled nearly every weekend with the American students. Silke and I did, however, talk about taking a trip to Africa someday. Another student on our floor, Gilbert, was from Africa and he told us about the beautiful scenery. He told us about going on safari and we thought we would really enjoy that!

My German dorm, *Theodore Wurm Haus*, felt like home by now and every Sunday evening after my travels, I returned by train back to

Reutlingen. I loved stepping back into the familiar kitchen, with its now-familiar German students and the bustle of studying, cooking, music, talking, planning for the week ahead. And I always looked forward to reconnecting with Silke at the end of each weekend. I would find her down the hall in her room studying or in the kitchen chatting with the other students. I would describe where I had been, sometimes resorting to our hand signals or I'd pull out my *Let's Go Europe* book and show her the map. She would tell me how things had been around the campus. We relaxed and laughed, sometimes over dinner or a cup of tea. This became my weekly routine before the school week began again on Monday.

Chapter 8 *Mari, Spring 1988*

Visiting Silke's family

I am forever grateful that Silke invited me one April weekend to visit her family in her village of Staig. They made me feel very at home. I went again to visit her family once classes were over in May. Getting to know Silke's family, her history, walking around the charming village where she grew up, really cemented our connection. Her mom settled me into the large upstairs guest bedroom that Silke and her younger sister had once shared. They wanted me to experience their German village life which was very much alive. Her mom, Mathilde, prepared a lovely afternoon tea party in the large sprawling, meadow-like backyard. We had *plum kuchen* and Chamomile tea on a picnic table in the grass, complete with a tablecloth.

As it happened, there was a piano in the main dining area of their home. While I had not studied much foreign language in my American upbringing, I had indeed studied plenty of music lessons. Weekly piano lessons since the age of seven, alto saxophone and church organ lessons were all part of my background. I had memorized several Scott Joplin ragtime pieces, which, I'm sure, sounded very "American" to her interested family. I sat down at their piano and played through my repertoire. Silke's dad loved my piano playing. He was eager to talk to me. He had so many questions about the U.S. He wanted to know about the culture, the people, what life was like there. I talked with him as best I could in German with Silke and Silke's sister, Selma, helping to translate.

Silke's dad had been born in what is now Czech Republic and came to Germany as a refugee at age nine. I thought about refugees. I thought about immigrants. What makes people go from living in their original country to actually moving to another country for good? It's a big decision—a big boundary to cross. Some, like Silke's dad, are escaping a very bad situation. My own grandfather was orphaned and moved halfway across the U.S. to live with strangers when he was twelve. There are many reasons people immigrate to another country—better opportunities for jobs or education, escaping a bad situation. For some it may be a desire to be near family or a different climate.

I saw that Silke's father had made the best of a bad situation. As a child he left very difficult conditions, moved to Germany, got an education, worked hard and made a good life for himself and his family in his new country.

When I was visiting the south of France, I got this crazy idea in my head to quit college and use the remainder of my college savings to buy a sailboat and live on the Mediterranean Sea. I shared my crazy idea with Silke. Of course, this was completely unrealistic and largely impossible. But it got me thinking.

Traveling had sparked my innate sense of adventure—almost like I dared myself to do something crazy that no one I'd ever known had done. It wasn't out of any danger or desperate conditions. It wasn't even for a better opportunity elsewhere. Sometimes when a person looks at their life they see traditional patterns, habits and expectations, and they want to break away. Living on a houseboat in the south of France would definitely have been breaking away for me.

My semester in Germany had made the world a much smaller place for me. I saw all of the people of the world as part of a greater humanity. We each have our individual cultures, but we are all human. I started to see the enormity of this and all that it meant for my life.

From my Reutlingen journal:

> *I decided just spur of the moment to write a postcard to Catherine Owen who was my pen pal in the fourth grade. She lived in Tokyo at the time and then she moved to England. So, I wrote her and told her I would be in England at the beginning of June and I would like to meet her. The funny thing was that I started crying when I wrote the postcard. It was happy crying. It made me realize how this trip was tying my life together and I realized how small the world really is and how much I am a part of it.*

Chapter 9 *Mari, Summer 1988*

The end of a life-changing semester

May 6 brought Silke's twentieth birthday. Throwing a party for your own birthday isn't done much in the U.S. However, in Germany, it's a common custom. Rather than rely on friends or family to plan the type of party you would like, in Germany you get to make your party the way you want. Silke threw quite a party for herself that night. It was held in the kitchen of our dorm. We had the music playing loud as she and I made lots of food. There were two birthday cakes. Almost everyone from our floor came. It was a warm evening, and people were out on the balcony, just outside the kitchen. Silke's friend from home came to visit. We were having a great time—until the *Polizei* (police) showed up. The neighbors had complained about noise. That was the end of a fun night.

After my semester of classes ended, my parents came to Germany to visit and the three of us traveled around Europe together. This was their first time visiting Europe. My parents had planned an itinerary with a U.S. travel agent based on my advice on the locations I thought they'd like. I got to be the tour guide now. It was a different kind of travel than I was accustomed to—no youth hostels or bags of almonds on the train. When my parents came, we ate delicious meals in local restaurants. We stayed in nice hotels and had a cabin in a real sleeper car on our night train to Venice, Italy.

Our Itinerary:

Reutlingen, Germany
Munich, Germany
Salzburg, Austria

Vienna, Austria
Venice, Italy
Nice, France
Paris, France
Luzern, Switzerland

They were delighted with the different cultures and languages. Upon their arrival in Reutlingen, I introduced them to Silke. I had told my parents all about Silke in my many letters home to them. They loved meeting her and made sure she knew she would always be welcome to visit us in the U.S.

Then in mid-June, 1988, after we finished our trip, my parents flew home and I headed back to Reutlingen to get my things and prepare to fly back to the U.S. I had a return ticket already booked with IcelandAir.

Silke and I vowed to keep in touch. I said a last goodbye to her before heading to the train station. We were both crying. She turned to go. Then she turned around again and said to me in English, "Mari, don't lose your way." I cried and cried on the journey home.

Chapter 10 *Silke, 1988-1989*

Life right after college is no fun

After I graduated I moved back in with my parents. I sent out my resume for jobs anywhere in Germany and what a surprise—Rainer, the boyfriend I had not heard from in three months, called me. "Have you applied for jobs up north? You know, if you don't move up north, there is no way we'll be together."

I should have told him to take a hike right then after all the silence and no letters, but I was twenty, my brain was not fully developed yet, and I was happy to hear from him. He invited me to meet him in Münster. From there we would see Hamburg. He wanted to show me the north of Germany. My parents were not thrilled. They had only met him once before even though we had dated in Reutlingen for about a year. People from the north are different from those in the south. They have a cooler temperament, a different kind of humor, eat a lot of fish and potatoes and are most likely Lutheran. I thought that my parents, who both grew up in Bavaria, just had a prejudice to the industrialized, liberal north where the residents believed the people from the south to be no more than hick farmers who spoke funny. My parents did not understand our relationship and how we inspired each other intellectually. And so what if he didn't call all the time?

I took an overnight train to Münster and he picked me up at the train station. He showed me the North Sea, we ate all kinds of fishy dishes, took a boat tour around Hamburg and had a wonderful time. We drove to the town where his grandparents lived but walked by their residence at a distance. We did not stop in to see them because he said, "They are private people who do not appreciate surprise visits."

When I arrived back home, I had mail from two textile companies that invited me to interview. One was in Bad Säckingen in the Black Forest, close to where my older sister, Margot, lived, and one was in Kassel, in the north close to the border to East Germany. This was pre-1989 and the wall separated East (communist) Germany from West (free) Germany. I traveled to both locations and found the city in the north grey and depressing and the more familiar south inviting and cheerful. Both companies offered me a job. The job offer in the south was in a textile testing laboratory within the company and the job up north was overseeing the textile testing laboratory and being part of the quality control.

After talking it through with Rainer, he pointed out that he only lived an hour away from Kassel and that he could come and see me every weekend. My decision was made! I was moving up north!

My mom was not happy. She was angry with me for taking the job so far away from home. Thinking about it now I realize that when I left home she lost my help with my father and around the house. The way I saw it, I had to start my own life, so I rented a little moving truck and loaded up the few belongings I had. My kitchen items were things that I had saved from my grandmother's. My mom lost it when I took my pillow and comforter out to the truck. We actually had a tug of war on our neighborhood street. She did not want me to take my comforter and pillow. She knew that Rainer would come and see me on the weekends and she did not want me to share them. In her eyes, I was going to live in sin and go to hell. It was embarrassing and I was so glad to leave.

Being in Kassel was a different thing altogether. The textile weaving company, Gottschalk, made auto upholstery fabric for Volkswagen, Mercedes and Keiper Recaro. They had created this quality control position because they were forced to by their clients in the automobile industry. No one within the company could tell me exactly what my job entailed except that I had to write a handbook about how the company was upholding the quality of their fabric through the spinning and weaving process. I also found out that I had been the only applicant for the position. Work relationships in Germany (at least at this company), were very superficial. Everyone was courteous and friendly—you might even go out as a group for lunch but as soon as your eight hours were over, the contact stopped and it was not encouraged to be friends outside the workplace. Kassel was in West Germany but very close to the East German border with its six-foot high chain link and barbed wire fence. Huge towers along the fence line held military personnel carrying machine guns. I could see villages and people in the distance, but they might as well have been on the moon. It was not a popular choice to live in the *Zonenrandgebiet* area, adjacent to the Soviet Zone.

I wrote to Mari and told her I had doubts about my decision to move to Kassel.

I was so exhausted after my eight-hour workday, that I barely ate dinner before falling asleep. And then another work day began. On Sundays I cooked food that I would eat after work throughout the week. I distinctly remember making *Saurbraten* (sour rump roast), and thinking life indeed is sour right now. I started to get depressed and wondered if that was how the rest of my life would play out. Weekends were fun, though. Rainer would come and pick me up, and we went out to dinners, saw different towns in Germany and Holland. I loved visiting new towns with him and exploring areas I had never been to. We ate the unfamiliar-to-me northern cuisine. We visited the North Sea and rented a roofed wicker beach chair (traditional Baltic beach chair), for the day and enjoyed spending time talking and walking along the beach. We had our textile education in common and we spent hours talking about work situations and how to deal with them or about the future of the textile industry in Germany. But then the weekend would be over all too quickly and the stress of my job and the undefined handbook was my reality again.

I went home for Christmas and Rainer went home to his family. We had planned on getting together for New Year's Eve, but he called me a few days before and said, "I can't come down for New Years. My mom just killed her boyfriend with a fire poker in self-defense and I had to drive to her to be with her!" "Oh my gosh," I replied. "Is she going to go to prison? Is she okay? How are you?" I tried to be supportive while thinking simultaneously how surprised I was about his dysfunctional family life.

After about six months of living in Kassel, he took me on a ferry ride and my first thought was how romantic, but that was before I knew he had planned to trap me. He told me later that he did not want me to have the opportunity to run away.

I knew that he had a three-year-old daughter with his ex-girlfriend, but I learned so much more on that ferry ride. "I have something to tell you. Please know that I love you and want to be with you. I need you to be strong now. We can do this together. When I went back to the north of Germany, after my graduation, my mother and my family put a lot of pressure on me to marry my ex-girlfriend. They said that I am bringing shame on our family. I have two children. My son is one year old."

My mind was racing, trying to figure out how he possibly could have a one-year old as well with his ex-girlfriend, now wife, but he did not leave me much time to think. The baby must have just been born when he started to date me in Reutlingen. He went on, "So—I married her and we live in the town where I work. My mom does not live very far away and helps out when she can. My wife was living with her parents until we got married. It was a terrible mistake. She and I do not get along and she is not intellectually stimulating. She used to work as a cashier at a bakery before she had the children. I asked her to move out and told her that I have a girlfriend, but she does not believe me. Please come with me to my apartment and meet her, so that she can see that you are not made up."

I did not know what to say, "Why did you not tell me before? What do you want me to say?"

He paused for a little while and then said, "I was afraid that you would leave me. I need you. I want her to move out and get a job before I divorce her so that I don't have to pay so much child support." I was speechless and thought, this cannot be my life. I should have left right that minute and taken the train home but instead I went with him to their apartment.

It was a small second floor apartment in a typical German apartment building. The living room was big though and the table was set in traditional *Kaffeeklatsch* (an informal gathering for drinking coffee and talking) fashion. Tablecloth, cup and saucers and, of course, a cake. She greeted us both at the door and at first the children hid behind her. She was a beautiful woman with medium-long blond curly hair, about my size, and had stunning blue eyes. We sat at the table and she brought coffee out and served me a slice of cake. Rainer talked the whole time to her and how she needed to go back to school, get a job and most importantly, move out with the children. While all this was going on, the little one-year-old kept on toddling over to me, repeatedly handing me toys that I wrapped up into a napkin and he enjoyed unwrapping. Over and over. It was terribly awkward, and I could not wait to leave. She did not ask me any questions. I think she was in shock, too. She kept on looking over at me and sizing me up, however. The whole "meeting" took maybe an hour. I was looking around the dining room that flowed into the living room and just wanted to disappear. I felt sorry for her. My mind was racing. He was demeaning to her and it occurred to me that if he treated her like that, he might treat me as inferior, too, someday. As Rainer and I were leaving, the children started to cry and the three-year-old shouted, "Daddy, don't go! Daddy, daddy, daddy." They ran after him. We ran quickly down the stairs and left.

When he drove me home that evening he made me promise to please stick it out with him.

"I need you to know I made a terrible mistake but together we are going to fix this. I don't know if I can make it through a divorce without you. I will kill myself if you leave me."

I felt like running away but couldn't because of my new job, his suicide threat and I felt like I should give him a chance to fix his mistake. It would look terrible on my next resume if I only stayed a few months in a new job. I could not think straight. Should I give him a chance to fix this situation? How long? Oh my god—do I want to be the other woman and a homewrecker? I thought about it for days.

Over the following months it came to light that Ranier's wife was not motivated to move out and he was unsure when to separate because in Germany in 1989 it did not look good for an employee to get a divorce. He had to think of his career. He had panic attacks, afraid that I was going to leave him. He would not only show up on the weekends but surprised me with visits in the middle of the week—which he never had done before. He also started to call me in the middle of the night to make sure that I was at my apartment.

"Hello?"

"Are you alone?"

"Of course, I am alone."

"Are you really alone?"

"Yes!" I said a little louder—"and now I have to go back to sleep. Rainer, I have to work tomorrow."

This went on for a couple of weeks.

I decided that I could not take jealousy on top of everything else and broke up with him when he came to my apartment the following weekend. He was furious. I got scared of him. "You will never find anybody else who will love you the way that I do," he said. "We belong together."

Then he grabbed me very tightly and pulled me violently towards him. He started to put hickies all over my neck. I wiggled free only to have him grab me again. I was very afraid by now and shaking all over. I ran to the front door but could not open it. When he grabbed me again, I screamed. He stopped. He apologized. "This will never happen again. Please promise me that you won't leave me. I will kill myself if you do. I don't know what I will do without you!"

I pretended that all was forgiven. I needed him out of my apartment.

The next day I tried to look for another apartment but in 1989 there were not enough apartments in Kassel for all the people, and landlords would not give me a chance because I was so young. They were afraid of parties. Simultaneously, I looked in the newspaper for women who were looking for roommates. I found one and met her, but she was a vegetarian and did not like that I was not, no matter what I said. I had no choice and had to stay in the same apartment. Stay in the same job. I went to the property manager and asked him to change my locks, which he did the next day.

Rainer showed up on Thursday night that week and tried to get into my apartment. When he realized that I had changed the locks he started shouting outside my window. "Come on, let me in. What is wrong with you? Come on, honey, let me in."

It went on for hours. I would not answer. I just lay there really still while he cried, shouted and rattled the door. Wide awake with my heart pounding so loud I could hear it ringing in my ears. How had it come to this? He was not the person I fell in love with. Had he lost his mind? Had I been so blind to not see this side of him? I was also really embarrassed—how had I slipped into this dysfunctional situation? What did it say about me to pick such a bad partner? I wrote to Mari telling her that I seem to pick the cheaters.

When he continued to call in the middle of the night, I had no choice but to unplug my phone. I felt so alone. I moved to this city—a four-hour car ride on the Autobahn, eight-hour train ride from my home. I did not know anybody but him. Had he done this on purpose? Separated me from my support system? I could not tell my parents. Their life was hard enough as it was. I was not going to add to their stress level. I don't remember how many times Ranier came and repeated the pleading outside my door, but I never ran into him again. He might have stalked me and I did not realize it. That is very possible. But I never saw him again nor know what happened to him, his mother or his wife and kids. That was fine with me. It really was not my problem. Except that my heart was broken and I felt betrayed. I wrote several letters to Mari about my troubled life.

I worked and took classes in the evening at the local community college to maybe meet some locals. I took English, meditation and an art class there. It was hard to meet people. The people up north are very private and so I was on my own on the weekends and took the train either to the south to see my family or to northern towns to explore the sights and visit museums—if I wasn't laid up with a migraine, which I suddenly came down with on the weekends. The headaches started with flickering, rainbow colored zicky, zacky lights on one side of my peripheral vision and about fifteen minutes later I had such a bad migraine that I had to go to bed with the curtains drawn. I went to the doctor and he said that I needed to make changes in my life. He suggested I quit my job and have less stress.

I wrote to Mari, confiding in her that I seemed to only find boyfriends who were "dish rags," that my life was not working out as planned. I loved writing to Mari. Even though it was hard to write in English, I wrote to her as some use their diaries. There was nothing hidden. My feelings were all out in the open. I felt that I could completely trust her. She wrote back that she was having boy troubles herself.

I followed the political unrest in East Germany. There seemed to be a chance that the borders would open, and people gathered in Berlin on both sides of the wall. It was very exciting. It was November 9th, 1989, and it looked like the Cold War was over. The spokesperson for the communist party, Guenter Schabowski, said that by midnight that day, citizens of East Germany were free to cross the country's border after being cut off from West Germany for twenty-eight years. It was a Wednesday night when the border crossings came down and by the following weekend, Kassel was flooded with East German Trabants—cars that appeared to be from a different era. It was unreal. The normally closed up, private people in Kassel opened their homes and the whole city was one big party of happy reunification. It was very powerful to be part of an historical event of such a significance and it was the first time since I had moved to the border town of Kassel that I was glad that I lived there. People were more open all of a sudden and I finally got invited by people in my community college evening classes to join them on trips to the former East Germany. We went to Weimar, Leipzig and Dresden several times and it was very interesting. The houses were all colored brown from the coal heating, like an old photograph. It was like walking in a time long since gone. The restaurants were totally overwhelmed and could not keep up with the stream of westerners but thanks to the farmers on the outskirts of town that made homemade sausages, we did not starve on our trip back in time. Not only had a border opened for the East Germans, but also one for me and my integration into Kassel.

I also wanted to break my connection with the Catholic church. The church and state are not separate in Germany. In Germany if you are Catholic, you have a required tax that supports the church. I had to pay nine percent income tax every month and that really ticked me off. You are also expected to donate money on Sundays at church. I formally went to a Catholic office in Kassel and renounced my membership. The clergyman tried to convince me to not leave the church because it would be hard for me to find another job with no religious affiliation in Germany—so he said. I had made up my mind, though. They were not going to get another penny from me.

I had to also make changes for my health. I read self-help books and I especially liked one titled, *Just do it!* No, it was not a book released by Nike. It was all about making changes to take control of your life. It suggested making a list of goals—for me, one of the goals was to change my choice of boyfriend. I made a list of things that I valued in a person I wanted to have as a potential life partner. It was quite a long list.

I was afraid that I had wasted too much time already. It looked to me that all my close friends had found loving partners and I was worried all the good men were gone and I would end up a spinster. I was twenty-two!

I applied to the Reutlingen University again to go back to school and add another degree to my textile resume. This time I would finally study textile design—my dream career. I traveled to Reutlingen and presented my art portfolio along with fifty other hopefuls. This required a day-long test, drawing fifteen-minute drawings of things that they put in front of us. I was accepted and now had an escape plan from my lonely life up north. I would continue my studies in the fall of 1991. I was so excited.

Chapter 11 *Mari, Summer 1990*

Deutsche-Amerikanische Freundschaft

(German-American friendship)

After my time in Reutlingen, I returned to the States and continued with my college studies at Valparaiso University. Silke finished her degree from Reutlingen Hochschule and took a job in the north of Germany. We continued to write letters back and forth as we went on with our separate lives. It would take about a week for her letters to get from Germany to my mailbox in Indiana. I loved getting her letters—she always drew some small sketch and even the paper and envelope she wrote on reminded me of Germany.

In May, 1990, I was about to graduate and had plans to work for the Lutheran Volunteer Corps in Chicago. Silke, needing a break from her stressful relationship with Rainer, wrote me and asked if I was still interested in taking that trip to Africa we had talked about. A lot had changed since then, but we were both adventurous and hungry to travel. I had loans that needed to be paid back and my volunteer job didn't start until late August. I was in no financial position to take an expensive African safari. I did offer, however, that I had time and a car. If she wanted to travel to the U.S. I said I would show her around. She accepted.

That summer, a full two years after we had originally met, our new plan became a reality. Through our letters and an expensive overseas phone call or two, Silke planned to come for a U.S. holiday in the summer of 1990. She was able to take one month of vacation from her job. She got her plane ticket.

I started to work on our itinerary. We were on a tight budget, so I wanted to stay with people I knew as much as we could (Airbnb had not been invented yet). And I had done a lot of camping growing up, so I knew that National Parks campgrounds would be a good option. I tried to think of friends and relatives who lived in exciting locations where we might be able to stay for a night or two. Most of my relatives lived in the Midwest, which I didn't think was very exciting. I wanted to take Silke out west. I got out the large paper road atlas from the car. I had been to Colorado several times and Yellowstone National Park, camping with my family. I loved the mountains and scenery. I wanted her to see that. I studied the map. I hadn't been all the way to the West Coast, except as a baby. I'd heard that driving up the coast of California on Highway 101 was breathtakingly beautiful. A plan was formulating in my head. My Aunt Sis and Uncle Andy lived in San Diego. I had only seen them a few times in my life. They were delighted when I called to ask if we could stay with them for a couple of nights. Silke thought the Grand Canyon would be amazing to see. I hadn't ever been there, either. My friend Doug Hahn was living in Portland, Oregon. He had taken a job with a technology company there after grad school. I called him and he said, sure, we could stay with him. Now I had several key destinations set up:

Leave from Kansas City
Colorado (because I love Colorado)
Grand Canyon National Park
San Diego, California
Portland, Oregon
Yellowstone National Park
Return to Kansas City

It occurred to me that Silke had probably never driven more than a few hours in a car before. The countries in Europe are much smaller and I didn't think she had traveled as much growing up as I had. This tour might be quite a shock for her. I had the experience of driving to Alaska with my family several years before. The United States is big. And we were going to be driving thousands of miles. I fleshed out the remainder of the itinerary, staying with other friends and reserving campsites along the route.

As much as I could, I wanted to show Silke the whole country, just as I'd been able to travel extensively and see many different parts of Germany during my time there. So, I purchased two plane tickets to Boston for the last week of her visit. I had a college roommate who lived there. I also wanted to visit Washington, D.C., to show her the nation's capital. I had a friend who was working that summer near D.C., and we could stay with him.

Silke asked in a letter if there was anything she could bring me from Germany. At that time, it was difficult to purchase products from other countries. I told her I'd love some Birkenstocks. I had nowhere to buy them in the U.S. Not sure what size to get with the European shoe sizes, I sent her a drawing of my foot. She thought I had big feet! She brought me blue Birkenstocks that I loved and wore for years.

Finally, all of the plans became a reality. Silke arrived in Kansas City on my birthday, July 9, 1990. We had a few days before we departed on our cross-country road trip. I took Silke to see the simple everyday places that are part of life in the U.S.—Kmart, the supermarket and the mall. I delighted in her reaction and looked at my familiar routines with new eyes. My parents were great hosts. We didn't know many people from other countries. My mom went to great lengths to make Silke feel welcome. She cooked German food. She cooked American food. My dad helped get my car ready for the trip. My parents acknowledged our sense of adventure, our unusual cross-cultural friendship, and most of all gave Silke a warm, Midwestern welcome. Even my parents' friends were excited to meet Silke. My mom's friend, Liz, sewed us matching pink-striped dresses, stamped with watermelons.

But there was some fear, as well. My father was concerned about the safety of two twenty-two-year-old women, alone on a long road trip. Of course, there was no such thing as a cell phone, or at least we certainly didn't own one. Wanting to give us some form of self-protection, my dad sent us with a ball peen hammer to keep in our tent in case anyone tried to give us any trouble. I also had a small mace spray that I had purchased for protection. We were told to call home regularly so they would know we were okay.

And so, on July 11, 1990, we set out on our journey with a home-made sign in the back window of my light blue Honda Accord that Silke had made reading *"Deutsche-Amerikanische Freundschaft"* (German American Friendship), with drawings of a U.S. flag and a German flag. I wrote in my journal on the first day of our month-long journey:

My thoughts are falling all over themselves trying to get out of my head. I knew, though, that my mind had not exaggerated that special friendship that I have with Silke. It is as if no time has passed. It is as if we were "sandbox friends" which is what they say in German for friends that you grew up with– you played in the sandbox with them. *And in unique ways we have grown closer without even knowing.*

Because Silke and I had had to learn to communicate with each other, it made every sentence, every idea, every conversation that much more poignant. We were forced to boil our thoughts down to just a few simple vocabulary words that we both could understand. But it opened our eyes at the same time. One of the beauties of a friendship that crosses cultural boundaries is that it helps you look at your own life in new ways. You can see things that are very familiar to you through a new perspective. It gives you a new appreciation for what other people may be going through.

We saw beautiful sights all over the western half of the U.S. Watching the sunrise over the Grand Canyon, visiting Disneyland with my fruit-eating cousin, Steve, driving on Highway 101 along the Pacific coast, swimming at California beaches and enjoying the natural beauty of Yellowstone National Park were just a few of the highlights of our trip. We thoroughly enjoyed our time in San Diego where we stayed with my Aunt Sis and Uncle Andy. They took us to an outdoor amphitheater production of Singing in the Rain. Neither of us had been to a tropical climate and we were thrilled to see palm trees and eat the lemons and avocados that Uncle Andy picked off his trees in the morning for our breakfast. We wore our matching watermelon dresses to the world-famous San Diego Zoo and saw the Komodo Dragons. Many people commented on our matching dresses.

The theme of our trip became, "I'm so happy." We traveled to breathtakingly beautiful, natural scenery, and to describe our amazing shared experience, we often just looked at each other and said, "I'm so happy."

But looking back, everything paled in comparison to the magical days when we pulled up to that handsome, three-story brick and stone apartment building on NW Flanders in Portland, Oregon.

Chapter 12 *Silke, Summer 1990*

The big American trip

In the spring of 1990, I called Mari to talk about our dream trip.

Silke: "Let's go on that safari and visit Gilbert in Africa."

Mari: "Sorry, I have no money, but I have time and a car. Why don't you come and visit me in Kansas City and we'll travel across the United States?"

It was a funny thing because I had no desire to visit the U.S.—ever! I wanted to see Mari, though. I had so many preconceptions about Americans and their culture. All they eat is junk food, they watch TV all day, are very fat and self-centered people. I pictured the U.S. Army guys walking with boom boxes in downtown Kassel, carrying McDonalds bags all the time. Every American, I assumed, was like this, except Mari. I really wanted to see Mari.

We decided after several letters back and forth that I would fly to Kansas City on Mari's twenty-second birthday. I was very excited and nervous because it was going to be my first airplane flight and I wasn't sure what that would be like. It was such a long flight and I was very, very concerned what I was going to eat once I got there. I was out of my comfort zone.

So, there I was, leaving the only continent I knew behind and landing many, many hours later in Kansas City with no expectations, where Mari (who looked very much the same), and her dad, Bob Johnson, picked me up. I was so excited to see her. It felt like we were just picking up where we left off. Mari's parents were very welcoming and took Mari and I out to dinner to Arthur Bryant's Barbecue—a famous Kansas City barbecue joint. The meat was good (I am German after all), but the portions were enormous. I could not eat it all. That evening a friend of Mari's brought over two mix tapes for our trip across the United States. It was so sweet—with music from Sting: *Message in a Bottle*, B-52s: *Love Shack*, Depeche Mode: *Personal Jesus*—you get the picture.

The next evening, Mari's mom's friend Liz had a party for us with very yummy, fancy, finger food. German and American flags were stuck in muffins. She had sewn us matching dresses—stamped with a watermelon print. It was not something I would normally wear but of course we wore them at the party. It was such a sweet gesture and I felt welcomed into their community. People in Germany often say that Americans are superficial and what they say is not really what they mean, but I felt the love from this group of Americans. It did not feel superficial at all. It touched my heart.

I brought a *spätzle* maker and my favorite Swiss cheese, *Gruyere,* as a thank you gift to Mari's parents. Mari's mom, Alice, suggested that Mari and I cook *Käsespätzle* for everyone one evening. Mari grated the cheese and washed the green salad while I put on the pot with water and made the dough. We had a lot of fun revisiting our time in Reutlingen while cooking together.

The next day we were off in Mari's old Honda with a tent, a cooler, two sleeping bags and Bob's hammer.

Looking back on it now, so many years later, it occurs to me that I did not realize all the planning Mari and her parents had done to make the trip possible. I am forever grateful.

We started our trip driving through Kansas, west to Colorado. This is when I realized how big the country really is. Germany is about the size of Montana and is the most populous country in the

European Union with about eighty-two million people. Wherever you go, you are never alone. It does not matter when you get up in the morning to see the sights or try to enjoy the peacefulness of the forest—you will always, always, always run into somebody. Well, there we were driving through Kansas and we did not see anybody. For days. It blew my mind. It occurred to me that maybe not having had any expectations was a good thing because I was starting to sense the enormity of this trip.

What I remember most about the food is how it smelled different, especially the Mexican food. The cilantro tasted like soap. I could barely eat it. The water everywhere tasted more or less like a chlorinated swimming pool. I could barely drink it. I had a sore throat from all the ice cubes in every drink that my German palate was not used to. We drink water in Europe, but it is usually bottled mineral water (that costs more than beer!), with no ice. Beer and water might even be served room temperature.

When we put up the tent at night we placed the hammer between us and laughed. There was always a lot of laughter. Now that I was in the U.S., Mari and I began to speak more English together, instead of the mostly German vocabulary we were used to. This meant we had to act things out which usually ended with us laughing so hard that we could barely breathe. We taught each other words, and speaking English every day was certainly helpful for my English language skills.

We either found campgrounds or stayed with Mari's relatives and friends at night but usually it was only one night because we had so much road and country to cover. It was really interesting for me because every state was very different from the next. It was like people lived in different countries. Each state has a different climate—

sometimes hugely different from the next. In Europe people in Spain live differently than people in Holland. But here they all spoke the same language—they were all Americans—yet they lived different lives. It was fascinating to me.

Seeing the geysers at Yellowstone was amazing. It wasn't just that I did not have any expectations about the States—the wild nature in between cities blew me away. To see a herd of buffalo slowly walking along and across the road right by our windows was breathtaking and scary. We saw moose swimming across a river, an elk eating right next to the highway and the amazing huge geysers, especially "Old Faithful!"

We had not seen a bear, so I bought a little stuffed bear at a gift shop for a good luck charm. We never did spot any bears, but we saw amazing nature and wild animals up close while in the car. The whole experience was awe-inspiring and something that changed my worldview and the way I saw America. It wasn't just a materialistic country, it was also a country with stunning nature trying to be preserved through the creation of national parks. It was out of this world beautiful.

We went on through Colorado and Utah to Arizona. There we camped right on the edge of the Grand Canyon. Looking down on it from the campground, it seemed unreal—almost like a piece of canvas. Mari wrote in her journal while I walked around and took pictures. The view was breathtaking.

We sang along to the songs on our mixed tape (top ten hits are also top ten hits in Germany so I was very familiar with the music). We shared stories of our heartbreaks and we told jokes. When you speak another language, you can understand almost everything if you understood the context of the conversation. My spoken English was getting better and better. Europeans hardly ever say that they are fluent. You can go to any European country and ask them "Do you speak English?" They will almost always say, "A little bit." Then you go on to ask them a question and they will answer in almost perfect English.

One day, we drove through an endless desert in Arizona. Storm clouds collected all around us. It got darker and darker in the middle of the day. We kept on driving and driving. It got darker and darker and slowly the raindrops started to fall. Then the thunder and lightning started all around us. The rain got heavier. I had never seen anything like it. We had thunderstorms in Germany, but this was something else entirely. It was a German thunderstorm on steroids. It rained so hard that the dry earth of the desert could not filter in all the water it was receiving. The water started to collect on land and on the highway. We could barely see the road even with our windshield wipers on the highest setting. We pulled over on the side of the freeway and watched the storm. We also noticed the water level slowly rising. It was very scary. Thankfully the rain stopped before it got to be a problem and we continued on our way. I knew that I would never forget the endless beauty of the desert and the thunder and lightning show that it provided.

Another highlight was San Diego. We stayed with Mari's aunt and uncle. They were so sweet and welcoming. I loved the warmth and being so close to an ocean. We went to the University of San Diego. Man, that is a beautiful campus. I had never seen such a beautiful university. How did these students get any studying done?

From there we drove to Los Angeles. We stopped on the way to get some beach time and I swam in the Pacific Ocean for the first time. There was an undertow, however, and it was hard to get out. It felt like being in a washing machine and we both struggled to get out of the water. Once we got back to the beach and toward our towels surrounded by other sunbathers, we realized that our swimsuit bottoms were hanging down to our knees because the sand had gotten into the little fabric patch. We could barely contain our laughter trying to empty out the sand. I said to Mari, "For a minute, I was a man," and we had to laugh some more. I am sure we were quite the spectacle.

The next day we met up with Mari's cousin. He only ate fruit. That was it. Fruit, no meat, no salad. That was a really strange meal plan for my German upbringing but hey, I tried to have an open mind.

We went to Disneyland that day and I loved it. It is truly a happy place. We went on many rides and it seemed that the resort had anticipated our every need in order to keep everyone in a good mood. Restaurants with great service, ice cream and live music.

From there we went to San Francisco where we drove over the Golden Gate Bridge, down Lombard Street and walked through Chinatown. I loved San Francisco. It was not only cosmopolitan, it also had flair. Next stop was going to be Portland, Oregon.

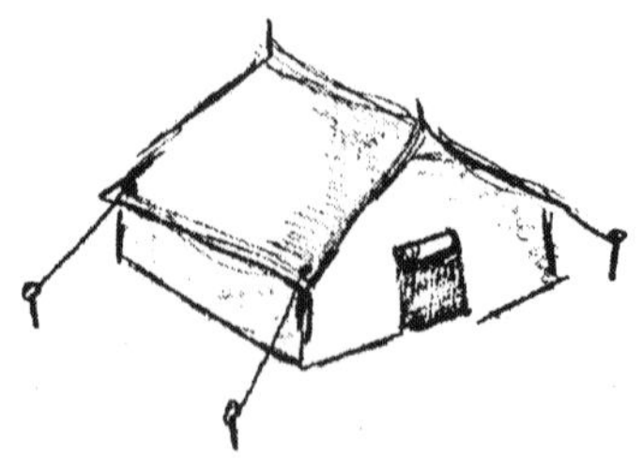

Chapter 13 *Mari, Summer 1990*

The weekend like no other

Remember Doug Hahn, my friend from college? He'd gone on to grad school and worked in the high-tech industry in Portland, Oregon. I had called when I was planning the itinerary and he was happy to have us stay with him for a few nights. I hadn't seen him myself for over a year, but in no time, we had rekindled our friendship. He had a roommate, Dave Monnie, a Portland native, who was always up for new adventures. It was clear right away that the four of us would have a weekend of good, clean fun!

Dave had a nice pick-up truck. It was agreed that Silke should ride in the passenger seat, so Dave could point out the sights. Doug and I rode in the bed of the truck, wind-blown and noisy. It takes a lot of creativity to come up with an itinerary of fun stuff to do as good as what we did that weekend. Humor, wit, inside jokes, indulging all whims. Ice cream, pizza and wine labeled "for congenial ambiance with friends." Have you ever gone ice blocking? We bought ice blocks from the Thirsty Two ice machine and then we had to find a good hill. Ice blocking is a lot like sledding only it's summer and your sled is a ten-inch wide block of ice. We all screamed with cold and sheer delight as we slid and rolled and tumbled down the hill.

One of the days we drove into Washington and up a mountain road to a riverside natural hot spring for a soak. And we even watched Dave skydive.

There was a record heat wave in Portland that week, unusual for the area. The un-air-conditioned apartment was quite warm. We made a plan to move pillows and cushions out onto the wide stone front porch of the apartment and sleep outside to stay cool. In the morning, when we looked over at Dave and Silke, Doug and I raised our eyebrows at each other. That's when I understood for sure that this fun weekend resulted in more than just a passing interest between Silke and Dave. They were taken with each other. The two guys were good cooks, too, and they made us several delicious home-cooked meals, which helped cement the attraction.

Chapter 14 *Silke, Summer 1990*

My arrival in Portland

We went onward to Portland, Oregon on Friday the 20th of July, 1990, to spend the weekend with Doug, Mari's friend from Valparaiso University. She had told me a little bit about him.

"You'll like him. He's very easy to talk to and a very good friend of mine."

That is all I knew.

I remember driving into Portland on I-405 and taking the NW Everett Street exit. Just entering the city felt so good. I felt the energy. It felt like coming home and I had never felt that about any other American city before this point.

Doug was there when we arrived. He was tall and skinny with short light brown hair and thick glasses. Dave, his roommate, arrived an hour later. Dave's eyes were very blue and sparkling. It was like he could look into my soul. He had very positive, exciting energy and an open heart. I felt close to him without even knowing him. It seemed like both of us were very much intrigued with each other.

The four of us went out for pizza on the loading dock terrace at Bridgeport Brew Pub, surrounded by old brick buildings and a view of the Fremont Bridge, which had a big American flag flapping in the warm summer breeze. While Doug and Mari had a lot to catch up on, Dave and I got acquainted. We could not stop talking to each other and even after the four of us got back to their apartment, Dave and I sat on the living room floor and talked until four a.m. It was as if time stood still. I was not thinking of the past or the future. I was all there in the present, enjoying the moment. The longer we talked, the more I was reminded of my list of attributes that I was looking for in a man—and Dave was scoring high.

When we stood next to each other we looked straight into each other's eyes. He had short blond hair, a spring in his step like a squirrel, short legs and a long torso. The funny thing we discovered was that he and I were the same height, but we bend in different places. When we sit next to each other on the ground, his upper body is taller than mine. My legs, however, are longer than his.

There was no time to tell Mari about what was happening to me. She and Doug were spending a lot of time talking in his room and when we were together—everyone was together. So, no time for girl talk.

The next day, on Saturday, we got up at six a.m., the boys determined to show us everything in Portland in a twenty-four-hour period. Doug drove his huge, comfy Buick Park Avenue with Mari in the passenger seat; Dave and I in the backseat. The car swayed as we drove, like a ship in water. The air was full of electricity between us and slowly, very slowly, Dave's hand found mine.

We started with a hike to Wind River Hot Springs. We had to drive to Washington and then scramble over huge boulders on the side of the river until we arrived at the springs. Germany has hot springs, too, but they are all developed into beautiful huge swimming pools with slides, and lounging areas. Usually there is a way to swim outside which is especially lovely in the winter when it snows. I had never seen a hot spring next to a river in the wild. We soaked in the mineral rich water and it was way better than any fancy swimming pool that I had been to in Europe.

On the way back to Portland we stopped at Multnomah Falls to gaze up at the majestic waterfall and feel the mist on our faces. These American boys really knew how to entertain out-of-town guests.

It was a hot summer night and it was unbearable in the apartment. We made a bed of cushions on the balcony and after talking for a while we all fell asleep.

In the early morning I woke up to a loud thumping noise. I realized very quickly that it was Dave's heart that I was hearing as he leaned over me and gave me a kiss. I was not thinking—I was just oh so elated.

The boys made us breakfast—hash browns with veggie benedict and hollandaise sauce—before we headed out to a small airstrip where Dave was set to skydive. By Sunday, I was very much in love. The thought that I was from a different country, five thousand miles away, did not even cross my mind. I enjoyed spending every minute with Dave and it seemed he enjoyed it, too. That was all I needed. There was only now. I had found my people.

Chapter 15 *Silke, Summer 1990*

The amazing weekend is over

Monday morning came all too soon, and the boys had to go to work and we had to push onward to Seattle. Dave and I kissed goodbye. He gave me a little stuffed animal bison and I gave him the little stuffed bear. We exchanged addresses and promised to write.

We were not even out of the city when I started to cry. I might never see him again. I could not stop crying. Mari listened and before we had even reached Seattle, we had a plan. I would call Dave from Seattle and see if he felt the same way.

I nervously called him, not sure how he would feel. My heart raced as I dialed his number at the apartment. This was before everyone had a cell phone. I might not reach him and have to leave a voicemail. I wrote down what I would say if the answering machine picked up or if I had to talk to Doug first. The English sentence structure is different from the German sentence structure. It is easier to write it down first and then rearrange it if it doesn't look right. Talking is way harder because you think faster than you speak.

I was lucky. He picked up "Hi, Dave...This is Silke. I was wondering if I should come back in a week and a half for one week...Is that okay?" "Yes, come back."

We both started to cry out of happiness. I would return to Portland for one more week. Mari helped me with my ticket. We had just bought ourselves more time. I felt an unquenchable yearning to be with him. I felt a pulling of my heart strings—it was almost too painful to bear. I just needed to be with him.

Later, I found out that after I left, Dave had gone over to his mom and step-dad's house and cried. They thought something was terribly wrong but then he told them that he had met someone and had fallen in love, but that I was from Germany and on a trip through the United States and that he might never see me again. His step-dad said later to me sarcastically, "What did you do to him?"

So onward Mari and I went to Vancouver, British Columbia (where they took away Mari's mace at the Canadian border crossing). Now we only had a hammer for self-defense. We drove many hours of the day and night, sometimes down to a crawl when we encountered a huge herd of deer and elk in the middle of the night in the middle of nowhere. We drove and drove all the way to Mt. Rushmore, through ghost towns, Wall Drug, Minneapolis, and all the way back to Kansas City where her parents welcomed us home.

I am not sure how Mari prepared her parents for the news that I would go back to Portland and she would visit her friends in Boston and Washington, D.C. alone, but I could tell that Mari's mom seemed okay with this plan, but her dad was not.

Chapter 16 *Mari, Summer 1990*

Silke sure is sad

Monday came and it was time to depart Portland. My grade school friend and her husband, living in Lake Stevens, Washington, were expecting Silke and I at their home that night. And, oh, the saddest change came over Silke as we drove up I-5 north into Washington towards Seattle. Silke became quiet. She had not said our usual daily motto, "I am so happy." With Silke in tears, and unsure what to do next, we discussed the options. I had already purchased our plane tickets to fly out of Kansas City to Boston and Washington, D.C., for her last week. And we needed to be back in Kansas City in two weeks in time for her to catch her return flight back to Germany. But she needed some more time with Dave—just to figure out if this was really as serious as she thought. They had found something special in each other and needed more time to explore what that was. We were eighteen hundred miles away from Kansas City and I didn't think I could drive that long by myself. Silke agreed to return to Kansas City with me to help with the driving. We made a plan to cancel her plane ticket to Boston, purchase a ticket back to Portland instead and she could buy herself six more days with Dave before returning to Germany. Silke's normally cheerful mood returned. It was good to see her happy again. We were now able to enjoy the remaining part of the drive—going to Yellowstone, Mount Rushmore, the Black Hills and stopping through Minneapolis on our way back to Kansas City.

She called Dave and I called my parents to tell them the new plan.

This new plan did not sit well with my dad. He felt responsible for keeping Silke safe. He considered himself her host in his country. He knew what it felt like to send your daughter overseas to lands you had never seen yourself. It took a great amount of faith. He had never met Silke's parents, but he felt a connection with them. He didn't want any harm to come to Silke. And now she was planning to travel back to Portland by herself to stay with a man he had never met. He was really worried about her and a little bit angry with me for setting it all up.

Silke felt like a total adult. But she wasn't in my dad's eyes. I was also a bit concerned for her. I did so want her to be happy, but I had doubts. Was this just a fling? How would this end? It did seem unlikely with the language and cultural barriers that this could work. A successful long-distance relationship that spanned two countries was not very realistic. But when you're twenty-two, sometimes the impossible looks like reality.

I wrote in my journal that week. *Even if it is not long-term, I hope it does not bring any pain.* I did not want her to suffer. I knew her history with her German boyfriend. Did Silke know how to make a better choice this time? I really hoped Dave wouldn't hurt her.

I went ahead with the original plan and flew into Boston. One of my past roommates lived in Boston, so I spent one night with her. Then I went on to Washington, D.C. where I planned to stay with my guy friend, Daren, from college. When I called to say I was in town, he stunned me by saying I couldn't stay with him. In the short time he'd been in Washington, D.C. he had joined a new church and had taken on completely new convictions. He explained that his new relationship with Jesus meant he couldn't spend any time alone with any girls or women. I was totally confused. Since his roommate was away, he told me I wouldn't even be able to visit him at his apartment. Unless we met in a public place with other people around, he was unwilling to get together with me. I was flabbergasted. We had been friends for four years and spent a lot of time together before this. He went on to say most painfully, about the time we had spent together before this, "That was in my past and I can't change it now." I took this as a complete rejection of my whole being. Why would a friend say such hurtful things to another friend?

This complete and sudden change in his attitude came as quite a shock to me. I took it very personally.

The upshot was I needed a place to stay for a few nights. Fortunately, my friend, Carol Jud, was from the area and although she was gone for the summer, her dad was very welcoming and even picked me up from the train station.

What is it? I cried out in my journal. Why can't I meet any normal men who like me just as I am? Haven't single people asked themselves this very question since the beginning of time? I knew Silke would understand my frustration when I saw her again.

Perhaps it was best that my personal troubles weren't to be witnessed by Silke. She was off in Portland, getting to know Dave better. I didn't want to dampen her mood. When we did reunite again in Kansas City, I only needed one phrase to tell her about my trip to the East Coast. "How was your visit with your friend from college?" she asked.

"That is not the love," I replied.

Chapter 17 *Silke, Summer 1990*

Back with Dave—buying time

Once back in Portland, Dave was determined to show me how beautiful Oregon was. He took me to the coast. Unlike California, the ocean is ice cold in Oregon, but we did not care as we walked hand in hand along the waves and collected shells. It was lovely. Growing up in the south of Germany, I swam in many lakes and in the "Swabian Ocean" aka "Bodensee," many times but being at the Pacific Ocean was spectacular to me. Almost unreal. The whole situation seemed like a dream. We rented the only room still available in town—which was the most expensive room in the hotel—I think it was one hundred and fifty a night and for 1990 that was a lot for people in their early twenties. We decided it was worth it, though, because it had a Jacuzzi and a fireplace. We made a fire and ordered pizza that night and he read *Jonathan Livingston Seagull* by Richard Bach to me by the fire. It was very romantic. We filled up the Jacuzzi and soaked in the warm water. I was truly in a dream state.

We drove down the coast to the sea lion caves in Florence where an elevator takes you down into the cave. When you get out of the elevator the smell (or stench), is unbelievable but after a few minutes you get used to it. I truly enjoyed watching these big animals for the first time in my life, laying and sitting on rocks, making quite the ruckus. It was a legendary experience for me.

Back in Portland, Dave invited some of his friends to the apartment so I could meet them—his long-time friend Joe, a sweet and very likable young man, and his daredevil buddy, Bob, whom he'd gotten into so much trouble with in high school. He took me to a band gig that he had in Salem where he played his trumpet. I met his mother, Bonnie, and step-dad, Ron. They lived only thirty minutes outside of Portland and had invited us over for dinner. They were very welcoming, and I enjoyed meeting them. I may have fleetingly thought, *Oh my gosh! I am meeting the parents!* but I was too busy enjoying the moment to think too much.

We took selfies (before selfies were a thing), on the balcony with his manual camera on a tripod set on a timer and had them developed at One Hour Photo. We hung out on NW 23rd for that hour, just walking hand in hand, petting kitties that we met on the way. We sat on a stoop watching people go by.

We did not need any words to know who each other was. I felt like I had known him forever, like I'd found a long-lost soulmate in a city that felt like home.

We behaved as though we had all the time in the world—just enjoying each other's company.

All too soon I had to say goodbye to Dave again to fly back to Kansas City. It was hard, but we promised to write and call each other as often as time allowed. We had gone to Saturday Market in downtown Portland and bought matching candles that we thought would be sweet to light when we were apart and writing to each other. He bought me a T-shirt that said "Portland, Oregon, City of Roses" that he said should feel like a hug and I gave him my favorite toothpaste "Ajona" from Germany, as a parting gift. We hugged for a very long time before I had to go to the jetway (these were the days when your loved ones could still take you all the way to your gate.) My heart told me to stay but my mind knew that I had no choice. As much as I loved Portland and it felt like I had found my people, I was a citizen of Germany with a job and a family that was waiting for me to come home. I wanted to see Dave again, but I had no idea how or when that was going to happen. I had no knowledge of visas or green cards, etc. Maybe he was just a vacation fling that I would get over in time...

Chapter 18 *Silke, 1990-1991*

Pining for Dave for 19½ weeks...

Back in Kansas City, Mari's parents had a goodbye party for me in their backyard with family friends, neighbors and old high school friends of Mari's. It was nice to see them all again and of course to spend more time with Mari. I told her all about my exciting week with Dave. She was very curious and supportive.

The table in the dining room was decorated with flowers, a watermelon basket, cookies, nuts, deviled eggs and some other dishes that I was not familiar with but I tried them. Mari and I wore our watermelon dresses. One of her parents' friends dressed up like a cowboy, lasso included. It was very funny, and I appreciated the extra effort very much.

The next day I flew back to Germany. An older German woman sat next to me who had been living in the United States for the last thirty years. Her mother had fallen ill in Germany and she was flying home to take care of her for a while. It was shocking to me how much difficulty she had speaking in her native German tongue and I thought to myself should I ever live in the U.S., I will not lose my German language skills.

When I landed in Frankfurt, Germany fifteen hours later, I took the train to Ravensburg to see my family. Selma still lived at home, but my older sister, Margot, drove two hours to see me. We made a fruit punch with champagne and poured our hearts out to each other. The next day we drove to a swampy lake close to our house and swam across it just like we did growing up. It was nice to be home again and see my sisters, mom and dad.

When I arrived back in Kassel, an eight-hour train ride, I had my first letter from Dave already. I was elated. We talked on the phone every few days and wrote many letters. I would usually say:

"Hello from your future!" because I was nine hours ahead and therefore a day ahead. Mari and I wrote to each other, too, but I wrote more letters to Dave—like every day.

It was lovely to talk to him and listen to his voice. I loved listening to his voice. We always ended our conversations with: "I love you. We will talk soon."

I would sweat profusely while on the phone with him which happens to me when I get very excited. He usually called me in the morning before I had to go to work and I felt like walking on clouds the rest of the day just thinking about him.

This was an exciting time in my life because when I came home from work and had a letter from Dave, that would be enough to get me through the next few days. It was also a time with very high phone bills.

A few weeks into our long-distance dating, Dave decided to come and visit me for Christmas and meet my family. I was elated! We planned on spending the Christmas holiday with my family in Staig. I would show him around the area where I grew up and then we would head to Munich, Prague, Berlin, Kassel, and back down to my parents' house.

Soon after, though, I thought of how painful it was going to be to say goodbye to him again after a short two weeks. After thinking about it for a while I suggested to Dave that I quit my job just before he arrived, travel through Germany with him for two weeks and then return to Portland, Oregon on the same flight in January, 1991.

This would give me nine months, from January to September, to see if this relationship was really what it seemed to be. I told myself that if it did not work out, at least my English would improve, and I would continue with my life and work on my Design degree in September, 1991. That way I would never have to ask myself if I should have checked this love story out further. To not think for the rest of my life if I should have pursued Dave with the sparkly blue eyes.

Dave was excited, too—so we started to make plans for my return to Portland. There was a lot to figure out. I needed to apply for a six-month Visitor Visa. In order to get it, I had to prove that my intention was indeed to return to Germany. I sent the U.S. Immigration office my acceptance letter from Reutlingen University and Dave wrote a letter stating that he would be my sponsor for six months, which I also submitted.

I gave away and sold a lot of my belongings in order to make my move out easier—however, I lived in a studio apartment and didn't have very much. I had to paint the interior of my apartment to get the security deposit back and give notice at my job.

The hardest part was telling my parents of my plans to move to America. My dad understood but my mom was not so sure.

So, the weeks went by rather slowly with letters and phone calls, more pining and affirmations of love. I received the six-month Visitor Visa in the mail and everything seemed to fall into place.

I told Mari the exciting news in a letter. She was happy for me.

When December 22nd finally arrived, I had rented a car and was waiting at the airport to pick up my Dave.

I listened to people talking as the passengers walked off the plane and had to laugh because to my German ears the American accent sounded like a whole lot of "r's" and "w" in a row:

"Rrrarrrrrrrarrrrr wrrrrwrr."

Dave finally got off the plane and we were both so happy, and hugged and kissed for a very long time.

On the on-ramp to the Autobahn, we had our first laugh because it read: "*Gute Fahrt*" (which means: Have a good drive), and Dave just about lost it, laughing. On that four-hour drive my vocabulary started to get more colorful.

There was no speed limit, so we got the manual out and looked up how fast our rental car could drive. We were able to go one hundred and twenty kilometers per hour which seemed pretty fast but there were a lot of cars that passed us at rocket speed.

When you get off the Autobahn, your drive will slow down significantly, and you are confronted with narrow single lane driving through little villages and fields.

My parents were really welcoming to Dave and my whole family gathered at their house. We had a wonderful Christmas holiday. My mom made a pork roast with dumplings and gravy with some carrots and peas on the side. Everyone helped to set the festive table with fancifully folded napkins, candles, and of course the advent wreath with four burning candles.

When my siblings and I were little, we had to go to our rooms after Christmas dinner and wait for the Christmas bell to ring. It was not really a bell but the start of our Christmas record that began with church bells. We knew it very well. My parents would set up the tree, decorate it as fast as they could in the living room, put all the presents under it, light the real candles on the tree and leave a window in the room open through which little baby Jesus could come in to bring us our gifts.

As we got older and my dad got sicker, Selma and I would go out into the backyard and take down one of the fir trees that surrounded our property, put up the tree and decorate it on Christmas Eve day. Often the presents were homemade, like new socks knit by my mother, homemade Barbie clothes, and one bigger gift of something we really wanted.

That day the tree was already there and decorated, all the presents were under the tree and there were a few little gifts for Dave. The presents were wrapped with wrapping paper, but some were in cloth bags with cords sewn in that tied. This way the wrapping cloth could be used again and again. I like to wrap all my gifts in cloth bags to this day. I sewed a bunch out of an old Christmas tablecloth with little cute Santa's on them and we reuse the bags every year.

We took day trips to the lake of Constance to see the Meersburg castle and Ravensburg, the medieval city of towers where I went to high school. We enjoyed the beautiful scenery, had coffee or café au lait in the pedestrian zone, listened to the street performers and watched the people go by.

Then we took off on our trip, starting with Munich where we went to the Hofbräuhaus. We checked out Marienplatz in the heart of Munich to show Dave the *Glockenspiel* (mechanical clock with dancing wooden statues) that tells the story of the marriage of the local Duke Wilhelm V to Renata of Lorraine. There is a joust fight and of course Bavaria wins every time. The second story showed people dancing. The whole show lasted fifteen minutes and then a golden rooster chirped three times and it was over. Millions of people come to Munich every year to see it. It is pretty hokey.

From there we went to Salzburg where we rented a room in someone's house and stayed several days (yes, people there rented out rooms before Airbnb existed).

We loved walking around Salzburg, went to Mozart's house and got tickets for a Mozart concert in the evening at the castle. We walked up Mönchsberg and took the funicular in the evening but got a little lost and walked some overgrown trails by moonlight towards the Hohensalzburg fortress walls. In the castle wall there was a ginormous ten-foot high door. We wondered how to get in when a little door inside the large door opened and a guy came out. We climbed through and were in. Huge torches lit the way to the concert. It was very romantic to listen to Mozart in a castle while holding hands.

We went to Prague where we had no local currency and the waiter basically lied to us and what we assumed was a thirty-dollar lunch turned into two-hundred. We did not figure that out until we got to Berlin and exchanged the Czech currency back to German currency. We were pretty upset but got over it quickly because we wanted to go on with our vacation. We parked our rental car in front of the Emperor William Memorial Church and off we went to explore the town. We went to the Berlin Wall where many people were hammering away on the wall to get the souvenir piece of concrete. We borrowed a hammer from someone and got a few chunks as well to take home. It felt great to hammer on this wall that had kept Germans apart for thirty years. Now we had our own piece of history.

When we got back, our car was gone. It got towed because we did not see a sign that was hidden behind a parked truck when we had parked there. We had to go to a pay phone to call the police and they told us where our car was parked. We took a taxi back to our car.

That night we could not find a reasonable place to sleep and we ended up sleeping in a parking lot in the car. It was freezing cold so we had to turn on the car and the heat when we got too cold and then turn it off because we were too hot. It was miserable but also an experience I never had before.

A highlight was Heidelberg and a ride on a ferry up the Rhine where we hopped off the ship when they told us that one of the castles coming up was also a hotel where you could stay overnight. That night we had dinner in the dining room with decorative knight armor all around us. It was just great, especially for Dave. The only room they still had available was a twin bed but hey, two people in love don't mind. We slept like kings in the castle.

It was hard to say goodbye to my family but on January 9th, 1991, Dave and I were on an airplane together and on our way back to Portland, Oregon.

We had a layover at the O'Hare Airport in Chicago where Mari met us and brought a picnic to the airport, complete with a picnic basket and table cloth. We sat on the floor off to the side of the hallway where a lot of people were walking to and from their gates. They looked at us strangely and smiled. It was so nice to see Mari again and enjoy her company. What a nice and warm welcome!

America, here I come.

Chapter 19 *Mari, Spring 1991*

Another romance is kindled

On our last night with Doug and Dave in Portland, we all sat on the front porch, thinking of the future, enjoying each other's company. We wanted this great camaraderie to continue in some way. Silke and I were about to drive away the next morning. She would fly back to Germany, possibly never to visit again. I was headed to a new job in Chicago, two thousand miles away. So that night the four of us made a plan. We decided that the following spring Dave, Doug and I would fly to Spain and Silke would meet us there. We'd take a beach vacation right when everyone was tired of winter weather. We talked about where we might go, the food and the sangria we'd have there. It gave us hope that we'd be together again at some point in the future.

Then, Fall arrived, Dave and Silke's relationship was blooming with phone calls and letters. They wanted to see each other again. They began to make their own plans to have Dave visit Germany. Then Silke wrote me a letter and told me about her plans to move to Portland! This was a turn of events I had not expected! I was very happy that things were working out between them.

By January, she had moved. There they were in Portland, the three of them, living in the same apartment on Flanders! Me? I was two thousand miles away! I wanted to be in Portland, too, enjoying the fun times like we'd had the previous summer. I felt left out, left behind. They were all moving ahead at lightning speed with romance, plans, their futures. I wanted to be part of the exciting life.

Doug and I had always enjoyed our late-night talks. In college we'd pick up a popular magazine such as *Mademoiselle* and discuss and analyze the articles, debating how true they were. When we didn't live in the same place, we had long phone calls. We solved the world's problems late into the night.

On one such phone call with Doug I said, "I'm disappointed that our plans to travel together to Spain, the four of us, aren't going to happen now." Dave and Silke's money were stretched thin, with Silke's move to the U.S. They clearly were in no position to take a trip to Spain at that point.

Doug surprised me and said, "I'm still up for it, if you are." I surprised myself by saying, "Sure."

We planned a one-week trip. I felt comfortable with European travel given all my weekend train trips around Europe when I lived in Reutlingen. We could enjoy ourselves without huge expense. Planning a trip was more difficult back then than it is now as there was no internet to research where to go or make hotel reservations. We booked our plane tickets through a travel agent, so that Doug would fly from Portland to O'Hare and then I'd meet him at O'Hare and continue on the same flight to Madrid with him. Of course, Silke's family wanted us to visit them. Doug and I each went to the library to look through travel guides. We had heard that Ibiza was an interesting place for a visit but our research showed that it probably wasn't our kind of vacation—glamour and nightlife weren't big on our list of priorities. We then learned about the island near Ibiza, called Majorca. The scenery looked breathtaking! The beaches and secluded coves in the photos looked more our style. We decided that would be our destination: Majorca, Spain.

Since Doug was doing his own research in Oregon and I was doing my own research in Illinois, and it was expensive to call each other, and email didn't exist, we didn't actually communicate a lot about our travel plans or preferences. Doug was taking the lead on this trip, researching the hotels in Majorca. I assumed he was making a reservation. I thought this was going to be a classy beach vacation, unlike the carefree student travel I'd done so many times when I lived in Germany.

My parents were quite concerned about my trip. They didn't know Doug. It was a foreign country. They didn't know how they'd reach me in an emergency. It was a different world before everyone had phones. I had been overseas for a whole semester, but that was a more controlled environment. When I was in Reutlingen, they felt comfortable knowing there was a Valparaiso University professor in charge and although he gave us free reign to travel when and where we wanted, he could've reached us within twenty-four hours in most cases. Our roommate or another student always knew where we'd planned to go, and we usually stayed at the predictable youth hostels. Plus, we were usually only gone for the weekend.

Anyway, this was a new level of fear for my parents. They insisted that I give them contact information of where I'd be and when. And I had to give them phone numbers of the places I was staying. I told them Doug was making the plans. I promised as soon as I got there, I would call to let them know I had arrived safely and tell them where I was. And I assured them I'd get them all the contact information.

The day came for our flight. I did some last-minute packing and tried to get out the door of my apartment on time. I didn't have a car, so I planned to take public transportation to the airport.

To get to O'Hare from my apartment, I had to walk down to the corner of Clark and Montrose and catch the Montrose bus. I needed to take the bus west to the blue line train that went out to O'Hare. The suitcases in that day didn't have wheels. This wasn't a bus route

I often took. And in those days, we didn't have a device tracking every bus and train—you just walked outside to the corner and stood there until a bus came by. Sometimes one bus would get behind schedule and after a while there'd be two or even three buses right in a row. Anyway, as I walked south on Dover to Montrose, ahead I could just see the Montrose bus pulling away from my corner, heading west, going past. I had missed it. Darn. But I had some extra time, so it wasn't a big deal. The buses on that route were supposed to come every fifteen minutes. Once there, I waited and waited. No bus. Thirty minutes went by. I continued to wait. Forty five minutes went by. FINALLY, a westbound bus came along (with two more following close behind—they were very backed up that day!). By now I was running quite late for my international flight.

I had no way to contact Doug. I assumed he was at O'Hare by now, on his layover, waiting for me. I finally arrived at the blue line train. I hauled my suitcase up the stairs. I waited and waited for an O'Hare-bound train. The whole trip should have been about forty-five minutes, but that day, took an hour and forty-five minutes. When I finally got to the ticket counter, they were paging me over the intercom. Doug was standing there explaining to the ticket agent that he'd flown from Portland and he was sure I was on my way. I handed them my passport and ticket. They stamped everything, and Doug and I ran to catch our flight. It was a stressful way to start the trip!

Once we settled into our seats, we started talking about the trip, the beaches, where we wanted to go. That was when I found out Doug had not actually made any hotel reservations. He figured we could walk around and find a place once we got there. I was quite surprised by this and let him know. What was I going to tell my parents when I landed? I was supposed to call them and give them all my contact information. We arrived in Majorca and then we walked around the beach town looking for *Zimmer Frei* (room free) signs. Neither of us spoke Spanish. But one of the reasons we had picked this island was because it was a big destination for German tourists. And my German was still decent from my semester in Reutlingen. I was perfectly able to navigate the transaction to reserve a hotel room.

But then we came face-to-face with the issue that we hadn't yet talked about—was this a romantic vacation? This wasn't at all clear. Perhaps it was why Doug hadn't made a reservation ahead of time.

I know what you're thinking, dear reader. To any normal outside observer, it would surely appear to be a romantic vacation—two twenty-somethings—unattached, adventurous friends who had known each other for several years, meeting up and traveling to an exotic island in Spain together. It does look like a romantic vacation. But all I can tell you is that at the time, we weren't romantically involved and we hadn't talked about what type of room(s) to get.

We found an inn with rooms available and the innkeeper, an older woman, spoke German—she was German, in fact. Her first question, "One bed or two beds?" It seems a reasonable enough question. I looked at Doug. He looked at me. He didn't speak much German, but he had understood the question. He said nothing. Since I spoke German, I was the one communicating with the innkeeper. I didn't want to assume anything between the two of us.

"Two beds," I replied. The innkeeper took us around to the various available rooms and unlocked the doors and let us look over the rooms, which was a common practice in Europe for these smaller inns and hotels. We chose a room with two twin beds. We reserved it for the week.

Now I had to give my parents the contact information they wanted. I found a pay phone in the lobby and painstakingly used a calling card (remember those?) and called my parents back at home. "Yes,

I'm here, safe and sound. Here's the name of the hotel. I'll be here for five nights. Here's the innkeeper's name and the phone number." I decided not to mention the innkeeper only spoke German and Spanish. My parents only spoke English. Fortunately, there were no emergencies from home while we were gone, so they had no need to reach me.

Doug and I had a lovely time that week. The beaches in Majorca were absolutely beautiful with their high cliffs and scenic drives above the ocean. The inn where we stayed was a short walk to the beach. The open-air restaurants served amazing seafood tapas and the beverage of choice was a pitcher of red sangria. Doug and I both enjoyed playing cards, so we took our card deck to the restaurants. On a rainy day we sat on the covered patio where we could feel the ocean breeze and ordered a pitcher of sangria and played many hands of two-person Euchre. The sunny days found us at the beach, soaking up the sun and enjoying the turquoise ocean water and salty air. It was March, so a bit off-season, no large crowds, the locals were friendly. As we got reacquainted and relaxed in this beautiful setting, we began to realize that there was more to our relationship than platonic friendship. Our budding romance began.

After our time in Majorca, we traveled to visit Silke's parents in Staig, Germany, for two nights before flying back to the U.S. I had not seen them for two years. They were happy to meet Doug. Silke's brother and his family came over to meet me. Her sister, Selma, stopped by to say hi. I played the piano for her dad. I always felt welcomed at their home.

Chapter 20 *Silke, Winter 1991*

Life in America

Doug and Dave had to go to work every day, and I was alone in the apartment. Dave had bought a Honda Civic for us and he gave me homework every day. When he was at work, I was to cross the bridges of Portland and find my way back to the apartment using only a Portland map (remember—no help from Google maps), to NW Portland on Flanders Street. It was scary, but I did it. His mom, Bonnie, had loaned me her sewing machine and I made baby clothing, trying to sell it in local boutiques with minimal success. It seems I was twenty years too early with this idea because now there are boutiques in Portland where local artists sell their work. Oh, well. I was not allowed to legally work in the U.S. because I had no work visa.

I cooked dinner each night and all three of us hung out in the evening and on the weekends. Some of Dave's friends would say, "Let's meet for lunch sometime," I took that as an invitation and would say, "Sure! That sounds nice." I expected them to invite me soon over to their house for lunch. In Germany you would not say that you want to have lunch with someone if you didn't mean it. So, when the invitation never came it was a little hurtful to me. Why would you say something and not follow through? Then just don't say it. It is funny to me now because it is just a figure of speech, a phrase to say something nice to express that you had a good time. I still feel like it is pretty easy to integrate into the American culture as a European but there are a few things that are very different. Another one is nudity.

When we went to a beach and I did not have my bathing suit, I thought, no problem. My underwear is colorful, and I will go topless. The Americans in our group freaked out just over me mentioning going topless or naked. "The police will arrest you." I thought that was terribly funny and to this day I don't understand why people in this country are so afraid of their bodies being seen or seeing other bodies.

Dave and I went on motorcycle rides, met his friends at "breakfast club" on Sundays at ten a.m. (my kind of church), and I also started skydiving whenever time allowed but stopped going after about six months because it was too expensive for me. Mind you, I did not stop because I was possibly going to die.

One of these days we went to the Blue Moon—a McMenamins pub around the corner from our apartment in NW Portland when the bartender asked me for my ID. Well, I did not have an ID because I was not a citizen. I showed him my passport and he did not know what it was.

He asked, "What is this?"

"This is my German passport," I replied.

"We won't accept that here. Where is your ID card?"

"I don't have one. I am not from here."

"Then you have to leave."

That was unbelievable, but I think fewer people travelled internationally then. I believe that he truly did not know what he was looking at.

On the weekends we sometimes visited Dave's mom, Bonnie. One day I went to the store to get some groceries and I wanted to also buy some flowers for his mom. I had twenty dollars. I shopped and added the amount up in my head. It added up to seventeen dollars. I had enough for a small bunch of flowers. I went to the flower department and found some daffodils for three dollars a bunch. When I went to the cash register I expected it to cost twenty dollars.

The cashier rang me up and when he got to the flowers he asked me,

"How much are these?"

"They are free dollars."

In the German language you don't have the "th" sound so many Germans either put an "s," "d," or "f" in its place.

He totaled my order and I gave him my twenty. He handed me back three dollars. He had understood that the flowers must be FREE. So, I was not charged for them.

I walked home confused and had three dollars in my pocket.

I did not understand what had happened until later that evening when I realized that I had not counted wrong, but that my pronunciation was the problem.

After that I was determined to work on my "th" sound and took lessons from my friend, Ute, who taught "accent reduction." I listened to tapes that she gave me complete with tongue exercises in the car. It really helped—although still not perfect by choice. I mean, I had other things to do than to practice my "th" sound all the time…and who wants to completely lose their sexy European accent?

On our first Valentine's day, I baked cookies shaped as letters that were a message for Dave. In the morning I gave him the cookies and

I told him that it was a puzzle. Except that I was telling him in German.

He came home that evening and I asked, "Did you get my message?"

"What message?"

"The cookie message?"

"Oh….I ate them. They were really good."

The message was: *Ich liebe Dich!* (I love you!).

All was well until one weekend in March. Dave was feeling overwhelmed. We had talked to an immigration lawyer who charged two hundred dollars an hour and after looking at all the options for me to be able to stay beyond one year, he said that our easiest option was to get married. Dave felt a lot of pressure about me being here—having left my home country and family behind for him. He said that he was not sure if he would be ready to marry me. "I love you, but I am not sure if I am in love with you."

Coming from Europe where people lived together for years and never got married, this caught me by surprise. I was not sure either if I wanted to get married (to him or in general), but I just wanted to enjoy our time. I also had my backup plan to get my Textile Design degree in September back in Reutlingen, Germany. This also showed me that he did not know how independent I was, and I felt strongly it was time to show him.

I called Mari and told her (while crying), what was going on. She was very supportive and in favor of my plan to find another place to live.

After he went to work the next day, I went out and bought a newspaper, looking for ads for live-in nannies or babysitters (no Craigslist yet). I was on a Visitor Visa and was not allowed to work but I could work under the table. I found two that sounded good. One was in outer NE Portland and one was in the west hills. I met with a mother in NE first. Even driving there, I wondered if it was a safe area. Houses looked not very well taken care of and most of them had bars on the windows. I was really scared because you would never see bars on windows in Germany. I went to the house, though. The mother was on government assistance and I was not able to work for her anyway because I could only work for cash and she had no money. I didn't understand when I had contacted her that she was not going to pay me in cash but that the government was going to pay for her home helper. She could not hire me because I had no social security number and was not allowed to legally work in the United States.

In the afternoon, I drove up into the hills in SW Portland and the houses were beautiful and the gardens were full of colorful flowers. Spring was in the air. Viola, the mom, met me in the kitchen for the interview. I told her my story, how Dave was getting cold feet and I wanted to show him that I could stand on my own two feet. She was all over it. I could move in that evening. I was excited to start work as a nanny (Au pair), for two very cute girls. Emily was three and Katie was seven years old. I was to bring them to school, oversee their homework, do laundry, some house cleaning and have dinner ready every evening at six when they got home from work. No problem!

That evening Dave came home to my packed suitcase. He was surprised and shocked. I told him that I was moving out. He wanted me to leave at least some clothing at his apartment for when I came to visit but I was determined to make a point and so I did not leave a single sock in his room.

I started the nanny job that same day and I slept in the family's home three nights before Dave stood at the front door on the morning of the fourth day with a croissant and asked me to come to NW Portland that evening and join him for dinner.

That was my last night at my family's house. I would work there all day—have dinner ready and then leave for the evening, back to NW Portland and my Dave.

I applied for an extension on my Visa to be able to stay another six months and looked into applying for a student visa.

It was a wonderful time. I enjoyed working for this family and their sweet girls, bringing them to swimming lessons, snuggling on the couch watching *The Little Mermaid* about one thousand times, getting to know the neighbors and their children and dancing around the house with the kids and their father, Phil, to Billy Idol's *White Wedding* when Phil came home from work.

Every once in a while, they went out at night and I put the kids to bed. One night, I was sitting at the kitchen table folding laundry and looking out the window. The curtains were white and red checkered and when I looked into the dark hills I saw a radio tower blinking at night. *OMG*, I thought—this is my dream! The one I had three times in a row when I was thirteen.... This is when I knew that I was where I was supposed to be. Chills ran down my spine, but I was content and happy.

Dave took me to his bank and asked the representative to add me to the account. The banker asked a lot of questions and was concerned about Dave giving his foreign girlfriend access to his funds. He said, "You know, she could clear your accounts." After that we joked about me running away after stealing all his money. He was twenty-five and did not have more savings than I had. We both deposited our earnings into his account and even though our earnings weren't equal, we paid everything out of this account. It was amazing to be met with so much trust and I was not planning to abuse it.

In late spring, we climbed Mount St. Helens about fifty miles north of Portland with Dave's friend, Joe. It is an active stratovolcano in the State of Washington. It erupted May 18th, 1980 and had had a few little eruptions since. We camped at Climbers Bivouac at the beginning of the Monitor Ridge route. Dave and Joe taught me curse words before we fell asleep in our sleeping bags under the stars. In the morning, we got up very early and hiked through a wooded section before leaving the tree line behind. From then on it got steeper and we had to climb over rocks, boulders, gravel and ash. At the end of our four-to-five-hour ascent, we trekked through a few miles of gravel and ash. Basically, we were going two steps forward and one step back. The view and the excitement about being on an active volcano was wonderful. I was alive and in good company. The world was (and is), a beautiful place.

In July, a bunch of Dave's friends and I went rafting down the Deschutes river which runs through the desert in Oregon. We slept on a tarp with just our sleeping bags at the put-in right by the river. I loved listening to the water, being with friendly people and looking at the stars. Coming from Germany, being in a desert was amazing and very exciting but looking at the stars in total darkness was spectacular.

To apply for my student visa we had to fill out a lot of paperwork for the Immigration office. They asked me if had known the whole time that I was going to stay longer. I thought, *do I have a crystal ball? No, I still don't know. I am trying to figure it out. I am trying to be with my Dave. I am not trying to live in America simply for a better life. There is a bigger middle class in Europe with higher living standards than in the U.S., with social medicine for everyone and six-weeks of vacation, plus holidays.*

And there were more questions, making sure that I wasn't a communist. This is very funny to a German as Europeans are mostly socialist. Germany is a capitalist country with a very large state-administered social welfare system.

I had to travel to Germany to finish the paperwork. Mari had a friend who gave me a free roundtrip ticket. That helped a lot. Every time I left the country, I was afraid that Immigration was not going to let me back into the U.S., and I'd be kept away from my love. There were so many hurdles to jump. We just kept going. Filling out more paperwork, waiting in the Immigration office with the unkind, unhappy officers. Sometimes one officer told us one thing and the other told us that was wrong, so we had to start all over again. Some people hire a lawyer to help them through the process of applying for a student visa, but we were young and unable to come up with all the fees. After a few months of work we were finally notified that I had received my student visa and I could stay for six years. I was going to study Early Childhood Education. Dave and I had all the time in the world now to figure out where this relationship was going. We were so relieved. Around that time I also talked to Mari and she had decided to move to Portland. I was so excited. The four of us could be together again.

In early fall, Dave and I took a motorcycle trip down the Oregon coast all the way to Los Angeles to meet his grandparents. They were lovely, especially his grandma, Gladys. They welcomed me with open arms and we had a wonderful time at the mobile home park which was very picturesque, right next to Lake Elsinore. I had never seen a mobile home in my life. I don't think they exist in Europe. It was very cozy and nicely decorated. I felt right at home.

When we left a few days later, Grandma Gladys made us sandwiches. At lunch when we took a bite we discovered a piece of paper in the middle of each of the sandwiches. It read, *Love you*! That lovely gesture really touched me. I could not picture that happening in the German culture.

During our time in L.A., we rode the motorcycle to see *Phantom of the Opera*. I had never been to a musical like this before and was very excited. The man at the coat check took our helmets and leather jackets and did not give us a ticket to get our things back. Dave asked for the ticket, but he said to not worry about it. He would remember us. The musical was out of this world.

On the way back to Portland, we stopped in San Jose to meet his father and brothers. We played miniature golf which I had never done before. I had a very fun time with his family.

In the beginning of December that same year, Dave told me that we were going to go to Seattle on the train for the weekend and to pack a nice dress. I was sooo excited. The train ride was lovely, and the city of Seattle was decorated for the holidays. We stayed in an old-fashioned *pension* called Nichols Bed & Breakfast—it was all so romantic. I was high on life.

That evening he told me to put on my nice dress and we walked to the pier and onto a boat for a dinner cruise on the bay. After dinner we strolled outside with glasses of champagne. Seattle sparkled in the night. We kissed, and I was just so happy. I know what you are thinking. Dave told me later that he wanted to ask me to marry him that night out on the deck, but his mouth did not cooperate with his brain.

I had no idea what was going on with him. I was blissfully oblivious, enjoying the moment and being in love.

The next weekend we stayed at the McMenamins Edgefield Brewpub which is a converted county poor farm encompassing a seventy-acre parcel of farmland at the mouth of the Columbia River Gorge. The European style rooms were furnished in turn-of-the-century decor. It was simply beautiful.

The next morning, I had barely rubbed the crusties out of my eyes, when Dave turned to me and said,

"Do you want to marry me?"

Of course I said, "Yes!" and he told me about his foiled plans from the weekend before. We laughed so hard we could barely breathe. Poor Dave. He said that asking me to marry him was getting expensive. He also said that he had not gotten me a diamond ring because I was European and not really a girly-girl. He said that he would get me one if I wanted one or we could go on a six-week Europe trip instead and we would simply get gold wedding bands. Well, that was not a hard choice for me: six-week Europe trip! (We went in 1994 just in time before I got pregnant with our daughter, Lucca).

I could not wait to get home and tell Mari.

Chapter 21 *Mari, Fall 1991*

Moving to Portland

Trying to make sense of my life.

Boundaries

Defined boundaries really struck me
Present and future. Here and now
Simple and complex. Truth or lie.
The world is out there. But I am miles from nowhere.
What are my dreams?
I must define my boundaries.
Ah. The pressure. Pushing. Breaking.
Hey, we are all in this boat.
And each day takes care of itself.
We all want to be free of the pressure.
Let's take each other's hand
And walk along towards our dreams.

Mari, 1990

My job with the Lutheran Volunteer Corps in Chicago was a one-year commitment. So, in August, 1991, my year was coming to a close. I reflected on all that I had learned at my job working in fund-raising for an organization that helped homeless people with health care. I had become close to my housemates Jill, Mark and Bogart. But Chicago wasn't where I wanted to settle down. I needed to move. I had no job lined up anywhere. I had no place to call home. I had two clear options: either move back home to Kansas City to live with my parents or move out to Portland where Silke lived with Dave and Doug. I called Doug and he put Silke on the phone, too. I asked them what they thought I should do. If I moved to Portland, it would be a big change for all of us. It was a leap out of my comfort zone, again. After all, I had only been to Portland once before—that weekend when Silke and I visited on our great U.S. adventure. I had known Doug for five years by this time. And it had only been a few months since our trip to Majorca. Doug said if I moved to Portland, we could explore our romantic relationship further.

I also looked forward to living in the same city as Silke! I knew we'd have a great time together, finally have time to do things together like cook. We were both drawn to creative hobbies. We enjoyed outdoor activities like hiking and going to the Oregon coast.

And, so, in late August, 1991, I packed up my few belongings in the Honda, (the same car that Silke and I had taken on our adventures the summer before), and moved to Portland, Oregon. I packed light—just my backseat and trunk loaded with my clothes and belongings, camping gear and a bike rack attached to the trunk of the car with my bike. I knew Portland was big into biking!

My friend, Carol Jud, came along to help with the driving. She had never been to the western U.S., and she wanted to come along to see the sights. We began the long trek all the way across the "northern route" out to Portland. This wasn't a vacation-style road trip, though. We were on a deadline. Carol needed to get back to Minneapolis as her graduate classes were starting soon at U of M. We drove through the heat of South Dakota. We had a great time camping amongst the bizarre rock formations of Craters of the Moon Park. We gazed out at the beautiful mountains of Idaho. We finally got to Oregon and drove along the great Columbia River through the Columbia Gorge. It is such a dramatic drive through the gorge as you come into Portland—beautiful scenery, the huge river right below you, with kayakers alongside ships, tugboats next to paddlewheel riverboats and picturesque mountains on both sides. You drive right by Multnomah Falls on the side of the highway. Occasionally you catch a glimpse of the majestic Mount Hood on the Oregon side or Mount Adams on the Washington side. It was a long drive but we finally arrived in Portland at the apartment on Flanders where Doug, Dave and Silke lived. It was so great to see Silke again! I was finally reunited with my friend. It was great to see Doug. I was so excited to be back in Portland. Carol flew back the next day to Minneapolis and started grad school.

I stayed at their apartment for my first week in town. There wasn't room for me to live there long-term—plus that trendy neighborhood was way out of my price range. The two software engineers with real, salaried jobs were splitting the rent.

I did have money in my savings account, as I remember it, about two-thousand dollars, enough to put a deposit on an apartment, pay rent and basic expenses for a couple of months until I found a job and got settled in my new home.

My first task was to find a place to live. I looked in the paper for roommate wanted ads. I found an older arts and crafts style bungalow in NE Portland that sounded good. A woman named Nancy, in her thirties, was renting out an extra room in her house for a year because her husband was in California in Naturopathy school. She had two big dogs and a hot tub. I loved dogs. And the outdoor hot tub was a big draw—it was a nice one with a wooden structure around it for privacy, just steps from the back door of the house. I paid her three hundred and twenty-five dollars a month to cover my portion of the rent and utilities. We shared the kitchen and common areas of the main floor.

Next, I needed to find a job. This was a frustrating time for me. I was twenty-three. Supposedly, my college education had prepared me for a career, or at least given me some direction on what type of job I should apply for. What was I qualified for? I didn't know. I had a bachelor's degree in psychology. A psychology degree can be very undefined. I had no job experience in my field. My time with the Lutheran Volunteer Corps in Chicago had been spent in fundraising and event coordination for a non-profit agency. And I liked that type of work—I liked helping people. So, without a lot of other clear options ahead, I decided to look for jobs in fundraising.

I found a part-time unpaid internship. I hoped it would lead me to some connections. I needed some cash until I could find a full-time job. I started cleaning houses and baking cookies for people. I also did a lot of babysitting. Silke had had some success earning money as a nanny, so I got some good advice from her. I worked part time for a company called Rent-a-Mom which set up short-term childcare jobs. I connected with a family who needed weekend care for their two adopted daughters. I stayed at their house for two days and nights at a time and planned trips to the zoo, the science museum and other fun, kid-friendly outings. I developed a close connection to those two girls—Felicia and Brittany. Sometimes Silke would meet me when I was caring for the girls. We both enjoyed being with kids. We'd sit and talk while the girls played in the park.

In my spare time, I got involved with some social justice groups in Portland. Doug and I both joined the Young Christian Workers. Silke and I signed up for a pottery class at the local community college.

That was a blast! We knew we'd see each other those two days a week, even if the rest of the week was too busy to get together. We both enjoyed working with the slab pottery machine. We'd start with a large misshapen ball of clay, place it in the slab machine with the double rollers, turn the crank and watch as an even slab of clay emerged. We also learned about mixing glazes and were encouraged to mix our own colors and finishes. Our ceramics instructor didn't think too highly of the blue speckled slab pitcher that Silke made. We laughed so hard about that! He also didn't give me a good grade on the slab tray I created. But that didn't matter one bit to us. We got a great kick out of the class and appreciated each other's creativity.

The pottery class was only the beginning of our creative efforts. We had so much fun together, we decided to make holly wreaths for the holidays that we then sold for extra income. We had some friends with a large holly bush in their yard. We asked if they'd mind if we cut some branches for a project. That was quite an adventure as holly is notoriously prickly! Of course laughter ensued, as it always did when Silke and I were together. We gathered the piles of holly branches and went back to Silke's apartment to assemble the wreaths. Once we had several finished, we realized we hadn't figured out where to sell them. At the time, there was no internet marketplace like Etsy and we hadn't thought to sign up for a booth at the holiday craft fair. So, we scooped up our wreaths in our arms, walked up to the trendy NW 23rd Street and literally sold our wreaths for five dollars to passersby on the sidewalk! Nothing could stop us! Now we had some holiday cash in our pockets. We headed over to a McMenamins pub for a pint of local Portland beer and an order of our favorite Black Bean Dip to celebrate.

People have asked me, when I moved to Portland, did I think that Doug and I would get together? It was definitely a possibility. Doug and I had broached the subject in conversation. He and I spent a lot of time talking and analyzing things. Moving out to Portland was a chance to give the relationship with Doug some time to develop.

But at the same time, I wanted to do things on my own terms. I wanted to grow up. I wanted to find myself a place to live. I wanted to work on getting a job in my field. I wanted to earn enough money to live on my own. I was trying to be independent of my parents' support for the first time. I wanted to become an adult. I had a strong desire to be able to stand on my own two feet. I was a feminist. I was passionate about social justice issues. I wanted to figure out what I stood for. I wanted to build a meaningful life.

Throughout the fall of 1991 and winter of 1992, Doug and I spent a lot of time together. We cooked together on weekends, either at his apartment or at the home I shared with Nancy. We baked peanut butter cookies and drank coffee together. We soaked in the hot tub in the backyard. We went to the coast a couple of times. Neither of us had a TV, so reading was a favorite pastime for both of us. I loved that I knew what would make him laugh. I was on a very limited budget, so we didn't go out to eat often or plan expensive dates. But we did have a few local hangouts. There was a diner that we loved to go for breakfast in NE Portland called Tosis Restaurant. We occasionally hit a local Portland brewpub—Portland Brewing Company or McMenamins. It felt so good to be in a relationship where we were both very comfortable being ourselves.

In December, my parents, my brother and their new dog drove out to Oregon to spend the holidays with me. Doug's parents lived in New York and he had a plane ticket to go visit them for the holidays. However, my parents arrived several days before Christmas and Doug was still in town. He and I wanted to show them some of the beautiful scenery in Oregon. So, we decided to drive up to Mount Hood, to Timberline Lodge. We planned to eat at the Cascade Dining Room—the fanciest restaurant at the lodge. My parents were paying the bill. Doug and I were in love, it was Christmas time and we all were in a celebratory mood!

Love was in the air! And in December, 1991, Dave and Silke made plans to get married the following summer. It was hard to believe how my semester abroad had started the whole process.

Chapter 22 *Silke, Summer 1992*

I do!

We set the wedding date for July 31st, 1992—this way we could say that we met on the 20th of July and got married on the 31st (two years apart but who's counting?). This would give my family enough warning so that maybe my mom and friends from Germany would be able to come as well.

We had about one hundred people at our outdoor wedding in the wine country on the outskirts of Portland in the city of Sherwood. My mom, Selma, and my sandbox friend, Tine, came. I wore a wreath of roses in my hair, and a short petticoat party dress with a pastel flower print. All the men in the wedding wore white tuxedos. Katie and Emily were our flower girls and the ceremony was in English and German for my mom. Mari was my maid of honor. I had never been so happy in my life.

An American Holiday

This is a story of a young German girl
Who came to this land on a holiday whirl
She came in her Birkenstock, T-shirt and jeans
To discover America and all that it means
She came to see Mari, her American friend, no one
Could have guessed where their travels would end.
The Honda was stuffed with their pup tent and clothes
Hardly any room for their fingers and toes
But off the two went on a wing and a prayer,
No-one ever witnessed a happier pair.

They headed to Denver, the Rockies or bust,
Grand Canyon and onward the coast was a must.
They rolled down the highway chatting and such,
They laughed and sang songs in English and Dutch.
They stopped to see friends and they camped overnight
Coffee at sunrise and latte at night.
They trucked up the coast from the bottom to the top
To see friends and relations, that's where they'd stop
No more than one night though in any one spot
They must travel onward, they must see a lot.
They pulled into Portland one fine Friday night and
Emerged Monday morning in a whole different light

In Portland two fellows were glad that they came
And not one of them will ever be quite the same.
That weekend was more than words can describe
For Silke was smitten now, love would abide
But off they must go, they had sights left to see
More miles to travel and places to be
Poor Silke was sad, she shed tears in her strife,
She may never see him the rest of her life.

It seems...back in Portland her Dave was sad, too,
His heart just as broken, as lonely and blue
She called...he was waiting for her to return,
They needed more time, they had so much to learn.

She flew back to Portland, her days were so few,
Before heading homeward to sort it all through.
A few months went by before David went there,
To spend Christmas with Silke, his sweetheart so fair.

Their love was confirmed, no doubt in her mind
She came to America, left her homeland behind.
They came back together to start a new life,
An American guy would make Silke his wife.
So that is the tale of this young German girl,
and the love that she found on her holiday whirl.

Alice Johnson (Mari's mother)

This hangs in our bedroom.

Chapter 23 *Mari, 1992*

Life in Portland

In January, 1992, I finally got a real job as an office manager at a twelve-bed residential hospice. Many of the patients at that time were young men dying of AIDS. It was a horrible disease and at that time the treatments were not very effective. It was emotionally challenging to work there. Dying from AIDS can be very painful and sometimes the pain meds were simply not enough. I remember one patient who was in his late twenties. During the last couple of days of his life, he screamed out in pain and also in anger—his life was being cut so short. His extraordinary pain took a toll on all of us who worked there, too.

My job description at the hospice included volunteer coordinator, fundraising, event planning, donor tracking, and bookkeeping. Looking back, it was quite a large responsibility for a twenty-three year old with very little work experience. My boss was the director of the hospice who spent most of her time managing the nursing staff and medical department. Among other things, I was responsible for fundraising, including a golf event. This was a challenge as I had never golfed or attended a golf event. I found the job very difficult. I did, however, enjoy the connections with the staff—they would stop in my office to say hi at lunchtime. The building was a beautiful old mansion and my office had a lovely leaded glass bay window that looked out onto flowering trees and beautiful rhododendrons. I started at a full-time position, but when I had only been working there a short time, they had budget problems and my hours and pay (which wasn't great to begin with), were cut to part-time.

Money was a big concern for me during this time. I had to be frugal. I had college loans to pay back. My Honda had rust problems and I was told that it needed major repairs or the whole engine would fall out of the car. I didn't have the money for the car repair. With my pay cut, I was barely able to pay my rent. I thought about asking my parents for some money, but I so desperately wanted to prove that I could manage on my own.

That June I got a two-month house-sitting gig, so I moved out of Nancy's place early. This helped me out a lot—instead of paying rent, I would now get paid and have a place to live. The house was at the top of a hill, with a Mount Hood view. I felt inspired then and my love of mountains continues to this day. I had the idea to turn one of the bedrooms into an art studio and take up painting. The house had a big, beautiful kitchen. Silke came over and we cooked up a storm. We made a big pot of split pea soup—Silke likes to add garbanzo beans and tomatoes. We made salad and dessert and invited some friends over for dinner. Silke taught me so much about hospitality and how to host a dinner party.

The housesitting gig involved a cat. She was mostly an outdoor cat. I had never had a cat and had a slight allergy. I fed her and kept her alive. But I doubt she would have given me a five-star review. The housesitting job gave me enough income to cover my expenses and I continued at my hospice job for the summer. By the end of summer with the housesitting coming to a close, I knew I needed a change. The hospice job wasn't a good fit for me and it wouldn't pay enough to cover my bills once I'd have to pay rent again. I felt like I had given the job a good shot. It was time to move on.

It was almost time for Dave and Silke's July wedding. I had helped Silke with some of the plans. I would be standing up with her as her

Maid of Honor. Silke's mom and sister and best friend traveled from Germany to attend the wedding. They came for about three weeks and I was thrilled to have some time to spend with them. Silke's family had been such generous hosts when I had visited their home in Germany. I was glad I could help show them around the U.S. and take them to some of our favorite places in Portland. We were all sad that her dad wasn't able to attend the wedding. Given his poor health, it wasn't possible for him to travel. I showed the German visitors around Portland and went on some day trips with them, exploring the area. They loved the Columbia Gorge and Multnomah Falls. They liked getting out of the city and seeing the natural beauty of Oregon.

Dave and Silke had a lovely outdoor wedding on one of the warmest weekends on record in Portland. It was July 31, 1992. They chose a winery setting and were married in a gazebo at the top of a hill overlooking the vineyards. It was a beautiful ceremony and I was so happy to be part of it. She looked absolutely beautiful. It was so special for me to think about how this all came to be—from my semester in Germany and our cross-cultural friendship.

The love between Doug and I grew stronger. He had brought up the subject of marriage, but I didn't feel ready to make a commitment. Not having my own career path worked out yet, not having any steady source of income and being far away from the support of my family, I had a lot of uncertainty and felt I hadn't yet found a clear path for my future. I really wanted to prove to myself, and the world, that I was an adult and could take care of myself. Doug was understanding. I just needed some more time to figure out my life.

When my house-sitting gig ended, we decided to get an apartment together. Dave and Silke got the Flanders apartment and got a new roommate. Doug and I rented a three bedroom basement walkout in a home in Northwest Portland. I quit my job at the hospice. I decided to go back to school. For several years I'd been intrigued by massage therapy. It was amazing to me that the ancient art of massaging tight muscles could do such a good job of relieving pain. I had experience with neck pain and back pain and I'd learned how beneficial massage can be. I learned more about the training and decided to study massage therapy at the Oregon School of Massage. They had a student loan program and I qualified for the financing. I was still able to work nights and weekends providing childcare and I still had house cleaning jobs to keep some money coming in.

That fall, I finally started to feel settled and happy. The anxiety over not having a job, not knowing where I was going to live or how I was going to pay my rent was starting to fade. I loved the environment of the massage school. It was like nothing I'd ever done before—experiential learning. The environment was so positive and emotionally supportive, especially compared to the challenging, emotionally difficult job I'd left at the hospice. The teachers were very warm and friendly. The course material I found very interesting. I hadn't studied anatomy before but I was good at figuring out which muscles connected where and how that affected movement.

One of our homework assignments was to get two professional massages from different therapists in the Portland area. I scheduled one at Carson Hot Springs—up in the mountains in the Columbia Gorge. I always loved driving up in the mountains and getting away from the city. The other massage I received from a blind massage therapist. A light bulb went off for me that day as I realized the power of human touch. This person who was unable to see with their eyes could "see" with their hands. They brought healing and comfort through touch. I was hooked.

I loved the classes, I loved the homework. I loved working on practice clients. I set up one of our spare bedrooms as a massage office. I discovered I was a very tactile learner and finding the tight muscles came easily to me. I was very excited about my future as a massage therapist.

Doug and I were very happy together. Silke and Dave were happy newlyweds. The four of us cherished the time we got to spend together that year, meeting when we could for pizza or a hike or a day trip to the coast. We all were starting to feel more settled. Life was starting to look up.

In January, 1993, on an unusually warm Super Bowl Sunday (which Doug and I had no interest in watching), Doug and I drove out to the Oregon coast. When we had talked about getting married before, I hadn't felt ready. Now that I was in school and feeling like I had a good career path ahead of me, I was ready to make a commitment. Doug and I had a good relationship. That day at the beach was magical. We hiked up to a spot overlooking the Pacific Ocean called Proposal Rock. The area is named for a local legend of a sea captain taking his beloved there to propose to her. It being the afternoon of the Super Bowl, there were very few people around. We had a blanket and a small picnic lunch. Sitting there on our blanket, looking out at the crashing waves, we talked about marriage again and I asked Doug to marry me. He had indicated that he'd been ready to get engaged for a while. Now I finally felt settled and confident of my future. So, it made sense that I'd be the one to ask him to get married. We rushed home to phone our parents and tell them the news that we planned to get married the next fall. We called Dave and Silke. Everyone was very excited for us.

Shortly after that, Doug interviewed for a new job which required a move to Santa Fe, New Mexico. He flew down for the interview and told me all about it upon his return. It was a great opportunity at a start-up company. He was very excited. I had so many questions and mixed feelings. Finally things were looking up and now this. A major life change. If I moved with Doug, I'd have to leave my beloved Silke and Portland. I wondered if I'd be able to stay in massage school which I had come to love so much. I'd have to say goodbye to the family I provided childcare for and Felicia and Brittany I had become so close to. I had never been to New Mexico. Would I like it there? At least they had mountains. And I had heard that the massage therapy and holistic medicine community was very strong in Santa Fe. Would we still wait until the fall to get married? We'd have to figure all of that out.

We talked through several scenarios. In the end, Doug accepted the job offer and told them he could start in July. That would give me time to finish my semester at massage school and we could get married before he started his new job. Then we'd have to pack up our things, say goodbye to Silke and Dave and Portland. The company flew Doug and I both out to Santa Fe to look for a place to live.

We called our parents when we returned from our house hunting trip. "Guess what?" we said. "We're moving to New Mexico in July and moving the wedding up to June." Since we were planning to get married in Kansas City, this was going to be a lot of work for my parents, my mom, especially. They were very supportive and jumped into high gear to help us find a venue, bakery, food, flowers, all the details that make a wedding special.

Silke and I flew to Kansas City a few days before my wedding and she and I had some quiet time together before the big day. We stayed in my old bedroom together at my parents' house one more time, just as we had the first time she flew to the U.S. back in 1990. So much had changed in our lives in those three years. We spent some time reflecting.

Because of our friendship, she had come to the U.S. to visit me and travel. We visited Doug and there she met Dave. Silke had left her whole life behind in Germany and moved to Portland and she encouraged me to do the same. She and Dave had gotten married. Doug and I turned our longtime friendship into a deep love. Through it all, Silke and I had relied on each other and helped each other be willing to step out of our comfort zones. We laughed together and cried together. We encouraged each other. We stood for each other.

Doug and I were married on June 12, 1993. We had just the wedding we wanted—outdoors at a beautiful Lutheran retreat center. We loved the setting—the outdoor worship area was in a wooded spot a short hike from the lodge. We crossed over a rustic bridge, symbolizing our crossing into a new life together. My dad and brother had built a wooden altar in the woods, so we could serve communion. We had a longtime Lutheran pastor friend marry us. Silke was my only bridesmaid. Doug's brother, Greg, stood up with him. I wore my mom's wedding dress, which we customized with beads from my Grandma Ony's wedding dress. Doug's family is German and with my love of Germany and our strong connection with Silke, we decided on a German dinner menu. It was catered by the local Valparaiso University Guild women. We had a keg of local Kansas City beer. We had lots of friends and family there. Many, including Silke and Dave, had traveled a great distance to attend. It felt like everything was coming full circle.

My friendship with Silke was a huge piece of the puzzle that had led me to this day.

A few days after the wedding, Silke and Dave, Doug and I, all went back to Portland. Doug and I packed up our belongings and prepared to move to Santa Fe. Silke and I bid a tearful farewell. I was going to miss her a lot!

Once in Santa Fe, Doug and I bought our first house. We immediately went to the local animal shelter and adopted our first dog, Foster. Doug started his new job. I started taking classes at a new massage school. We joined a new church. We started our married life in a new community where we didn't know anyone. We were stepping out of our comfort zones once again, crossing more boundaries. But this time, I had a lot of experience and I had confidence in the future.

Chapter 24

Mari, 2018

Mari reflects back

Feel the fear and do it anyway.

There are many ways for people to get stuck in life. Perhaps a location doesn't suit. Some are stuck in a job they hate and can't see a way out. Some people are stuck in relationships that no longer bring them joy or worse, cause them pain. Some are stuck in their ways—their thoughts or habits are in a rut and they are unable to open their eyes to a new way. Some people are stuck with money—whether you have too little or a lot, money doesn't buy happiness.

When I was a teen, I was stuck in some frustrating patterns with my relationships with guys. When I look back or read my old journals, I realize that during my teenage years and in college, I was looking for connection and approval from boys. I wanted so much to be loved. I placed my self-worth in the hands of other people—people who were consumed with figuring out their own struggles. I placed too much emphasis on their rejection.

I had started to believe that there was something wrong with me—that somehow it was my fault. But as I matured, I realized I didn't need a guy to be happy. Eventually, in my journals from 1990, that's the point I had reached. I was no longer stuck. Once I felt more self-confident and independent, not needing anyone else's approval to be happy, I was able to be more authentic. With Doug, I could be myself and he could be himself. Our relationship was not complicated. It was comfortable and satisfying.

For every way that you can be stuck, there are numerous ways to free yourself from the pattern. Here are some I have found to be helpful:

1) Be open to change. You don't have to jump at every opportunity to change your life, but hold a space to look at new ideas with an open mind. Think of possibilities instead of all the reasons to stay with the old way.

2) Travel. It doesn't have to be around the world. Your trip doesn't have to be a whole semester or cost a fortune. Get a *Let's Go!* travel guide and start making a plan. Take a long weekend and pick a new place you haven't seen before. Could be on the shore of a secluded lake or in the midst of a bustling city.

3) Get outside and enjoy natural beauty. For me, I love the mountains most of all. But even a nearby park or river or lake will work just fine. Tune in to the sights and sounds of nature.

4) Find your passions and make the time and space in your life to enjoy them regularly. Do you like knitting? Do you like dogs? Do you like zombie paintball? It doesn't matter what it is. Make some time to do what you love as often as you are able.

5) Question things. What did your parents teach you? Did you grow up with a certain faith tradition? Were there expectations placed on you for your line of work or who you should love? Do those ways of thinking work for you? Maybe they do. But if they don't, find some supportive people to help you step into some new ways of looking at the world.

6) Never stop learning. Read books, listen to people, take a class. Better yet, teach a class—you will learn much more from the students when you're the teacher. Education makes the world a smaller place.

7) Be grateful for what you have. Find the gratitude in simple every-day moments. There is always some little spark of hope, even in desperate situations. The more you look for it, the more you focus on the good in everyone. And remember, there is always good in yourself. Find the beauty, find the joy, and be grateful to be alive.

8) Eat real food. You don't have to get fancy. Learn to make a couple favorite meals with real ingredients, not the packaged junk that fills the shelves of the stores these days. Remember, a good home-cooked meal can change someone's life—especially if it is *Käsespätzle* with onions.

Silke and I love telling our story over and over—a story of international travel, coming of age, taking risks, getting outside your comfort zone, creating possibilities, finding your passion, crossing many boundaries. I love that one friendship has made the world a smaller place for many people. Whenever I go to Portland for a visit, I'm known as "the person who introduced Dave and Silke." I love this story because it has brought out the best in me. It brought out the best in Silke. It helped us to find meaning in life.

Things I learned in Germany:

– *Take a shower every other day, instead of every day*
– *Grow out my leg and underarm hair*
– *Bring a gift when you're invited for dinner or for the weekend*
– *Take a break in the afternoon for tea and cake, preferably with a friend*
– *Prioritize home cooking on a daily basis*
– *Slow down and sit down for meals*
– *Have unstructured free time*
– *Plan food/meals/grocery shopping*
– *Be in charge of my own money and spending*
– *An attitude that my life is going to be what I make of it*

– *Enjoy the simple things in life—understanding the conversation, finding the right bus, looking at the flowers on my walk into town, a letter from my mom*

I still love to travel—I love to explore the natural beauty of a place, meet the people, eat the food, try the beer, taste the local wine. I like to find out what people love, what makes them tick. I like to learn what brings meaning to people's lives. I like to see the world with a different perspective for a few days. I like to look at my own life with a new perspective. If you travel, you just might find, as my dad wrote to me all those years ago, that you can see how different but how very much people are alike the world over. Most would like only peace and love in their lives.

And when you go on your next adventure, take comfort in knowing (with your ball peen hammer for protection), there is no limit to where you can go and to the love you might find along the way.

Chapter 25 *Silke, 2018*

Silke reflects back

Life and where it takes us is a funny thing. I definitely believe in destiny and even if you don't believe in it—you will have to agree that Mari and I were supposed to meet each other. There were just too many obstacles and boundaries to overcome. Why did we go through all the trouble of moving across the Atlantic Ocean, across America? If not for a sense of life purpose or pushing through fear, seeing it in your own mind's eye as an adventure? What is your passion? What brings you joy?

Taking risks and traveling will make you see this world in a whole different light. There is nothing wrong with being content within your four walls or staying in the village that you grew up in, if that is what brings you joy.

I had a friend who was a boy when I was about fifteen that I loved to ballroom dance with but he said to me once, "I was born in this village and I am going to die in this village." His parent's house was across from the graveyard (just saying). I really liked this boy, but I could not see myself dating him, because what I knew about myself was that I did not want to know where I was going to die.

Dave grew up in Portland, still lives there and has no desire to move but he is an adventurous person, always open to new ideas. Life is never boring if you are with Dave. We created a beautiful home for ourselves, live close to his mom and a lot of our friends bought houses within walking distance from us. We are all raising or have raised our families in our cute neighborhood on the edge of

Portland, close to the Willamette River. We love our family, our community, our lives and our home.

My dad used to say: *"Aren't you glad we built a house right here?"* What he really meant, I think, was isn't it nice to have a cozy place where you feel safe? Gratitude for what you have wherever you are.

I try to be grateful every day (does not work every day—but most days), for how rich my life is. There is so much to be thankful for: the color of flowers, the smell of good food, sparkly blue eyes, the feeling of a love bubble when you look at your children or your husband.

There is no day that I am not grateful for my legs, eyes and ears. My father lost all of these things that most of us take for granted—I feel like I have to enjoy it for me and him.

I will be forever grateful to Mari for visiting Doug on our trip and delivering me to Dave.

Long term relationships take work, but we give each other room to grow and to pursue our passions. Dave's is music and playing in front of people is what gives him joy (Ural Thomas & The Pain—soul music—check them out online at *www.uralthomasandthepain.com*). Mine is cooking, sewing, gardening, painting, writing, dancing and herbalism. We share the love for trav-el and being outdoors either hiking, backpacking, downhill or cross country skiing, kayaking, mountain biking, or rafting.

Every day, I look at Dave and there will be something he says, does or just the way he is that makes me fall in love with him all over again.

So take that trip, eat that cake, cross that boundary—go for it and enjoy the journey!

Silke's Family Recipes

Homemade Herbes de Provence

I used this herb blend in a lot of dishes in college and to this day. Make this recipe and enjoy how it transfers your kitchen to the south of France or to the student dorm in Reutlingen.

- 2 Tbsp dried thyme
- 2 Tbsp dried rosemary
- 2 Tbsp fennel seeds
- 2 Tbsp dried basil
- 2 Tbsp dried lavender flowers
- 2 Tbsp dried parsley
- 1 Tbsp dried oregano
- 1 Tsp dried tarragon
- 1 Tsp marjoram
- 3 Tbsp savory

Mix all ingredients in a bowl. Store in an airtight container

German Wurstsalat (Sausage Salad)

This salad is a favorite meal in the south of Germany but also in Austria and Switzerland.

I ate it a lot growing up for lunch or dinner.

- 3 cups of sausages (boiled sausage like Regensburger, Lyoner or Fleischwurst) cut into julienne (long, thin) strips.
- 1 medium onion finely chopped
- 3-4 pickles cut lengthwise into spears
- 5 oz Emmentaler cheese (cut into small strips)

Salad dressing for Wurstsalat

- 2 Tbsp olive oil
- 3 Tbsp white wine vinegar
- 4 Tbsp brine from the pickles
- 2 tsp chives
- salt and pepper to taste

In a small bowl combine the salad dressing ingredients. Set aside. In a larger bowl, toss together sausage strips, chopped onion, pickles and cheese. Pour the liquid over the salad.

Mix well. Season with salt and pepper to taste. Cover and refrigerate for 1-2 hours before serving. Serve cold.

Bread on the side (and maybe a beer).

Käsespätzle Recipe:

This is Käsespätzle—the homemade German version of macaroni & cheese that I grew up with. It is a traditional meal in Swabia, in Southern Germany, Switzerland and Austria. It is my daughter, Lucca's, favorite dish. Feeds 4

- 3 cups all-purpose white flour
- a pinch of salt
- 4 eggs, beaten
- 1 cup water/ more if needed
- 2 medium sized onions, cut into rings
- 1½ cups shredded Gruyere Swiss cheese (cave aged)
- 2 Tbsp of oil for frying onions

Heat oil in a large frying pan, add the sliced onions and cook over medium heat for about 10-15 minutes or until onions turn golden brown, stirring often. Sprinkle with a little salt to help with the caramelizing. Set aside.

Grate the cheese and put it aside.

With an electric mixer beat the eggs and salt in a large bowl. Add water and ½ cup flour at the time slowly while mixer is running. Once the batter looks smooth and develops bubbles, beat it for a few minutes on high. The dough should not be runny, but soft enough to easily go through the spätzle maker (like pancake dough) You can add more water if it is too dry.

Bring a large pot of salted water to a boil then reduce heat. The water should simmer throughout the whole process.

Continued...

Carefully put spätzle maker on pot over the boiling water. Place about 1 cup of the batter into the spätzle maker and press or glide it into the simmering hot water. Bring them to a boil. Then return to medium heat. Cook them for an additional 2 minutes until they all float on the surface and remove them with a slotted spoon into a large bowl. Salt and pepper to taste and a little cheese. Continue cooking batches of noodles until all batter and cheese is used.

Mix the cheesy noodle with two spoons.

Add the onions on top of the noodles or serve on the side.

It goes well with a green or Chinese cabbage salad with a vinaigrette dressing.

Tine's Famous Cheesecake (*Sahnequarktorte*)

My friend Tine used to make this for all my birthdays. It is still one of my favorite cakes. It is a German-style two layer cake with a delicious creamy filling in the middle.

Cake ingredients:

- 4 eggs
- 4 Tbsp warm water
- ½ cup sugar
- 1 tsp vanilla or 1 package vanilla sugar
- 2 cups flour
- 2 tsp baking powder

Preheat over to 350 degrees.

Put eggs, water, sugar and vanilla or vanilla sugar in a bowl and beat them with an electric mixer until the mixture is very frothy and creamy (10-15 min).

Mix the flour and baking powder in a separate bowl.

Fold the flour mixture into the egg mixture.

Grease a 10-inch springform pan. Pour batter into springform pan.

Bake at 350 F for 25 to 30 minutes center is firm and a wooden toothpick inserted into the center comes out clean.

Let it cool on wire rack for 10 minutes, then after running a thin blade around the edge, remove the springform ring. Cut cake with serrated knife in half horizontally and transfer the top half to parchment paper.

Filling ingredients:

- 6 Tbsp cold water
- 2 packages gelatin
- 2 cups whipped heavy whipping cream
- 2 cups plain greek yogurt
- 1 lemon, zested and juiced
- ⅔ cup granulated sugar

Put 6 Tbsp cold water into a saucepan. Mix in gelatin powder and let it sit for about 10 minutes.

Whip cream until it gets stiff.

In another bowl mix the yogurt, sugar, lemon zest and juice.

Heat the gelatin on low heat until it liquifies. Stir a few times. Let it cool a little. With a hand mixer, slowly add the gelatin water into the

Continued..

yogurt mixture, then fold in the whipped cream. Put into refrigerator for 15 minutes (no longer) to firm.

Assembling the cake:

Re-attach the springform sides to the lower half of the cake. Spoon yogurt/cream filling onto bottom cake layer. Place top layer of cake onto the filling.

Cover with plastic wrap and refrigerate for a minimum of 4 hours.

Remove springform ring and dust the top with powdered sugar before serving.

Mathilde's German Sauerbraten and Red Cabbage

My mom was an amazing cook. I loved eating her sour rump roast. The whole house would smell of meat and spices. Makes me hungry just thinking about it.

- 3 pounds beef rump roast
- 2 slices of sliced uncooked bacon
- 2 large finely chopped onions
- 2 medium diced carrots
- 1 sliced cleaned leek
- 1 cup red wine vinegar
- 2 cups of red wine
- 1 cup water
- 1 tablespoon salt
- 1 tablespoon ground black pepper
- 8 peppercorns

- 1 little twig of rosemary

- 1 tablespoon white sugar
- 10 cloves or more ;)
- 8 Juniper berries
- 2 tablespoons vegetable oil
- 2 bay leaves

Place beef rump roast, onions, vinegar, water, wine, salt and pepper corns, sugar, cloves, rosemary twig, juniper berries and bay leaves in large bowl. Cover and refrigerate for three days. Check on meat daily and turn in marinade. Remove after three days and save marinade.

Season meat with salt and pepper and cut little indentations into roast to insert the bacon. Fry the roast in a large pot in the vegetable oil on all sides to keep the juices in.

Pour reserved marinade over the beef—pick out juniper berries and rosemary twigs, add carrots and leek and cook in slow cooker on high for 8 hours).

Remove roast and slice it against the grain into serving size pieces.

Puree the marinade with a blender (all the onions, carrots and leek should make it almost gravy consistency).

Put 2 tablespoons of flour in a canning jar and ¼ cup of water. Close the lid and shake until blended and not lumpy.

Blend the flour mixture into the marinade and mix constantly with a whisk on high until it has the desired gravy consistency.

Red Cabbage (Traditional German cooked cabbage)

- 2 lbs. of red cabbage,, core removed, halved and sliced
- 2 Granny Smith apples
- 1 large chopped onion
- ¼ cup bacon fat
- 4 cloves
- salt and pepper to taste
- 3 tablespoons of sugar
- 5 tablespoons of red wine vinegar
- 1 cup of red wine
- 1 bay leaf

Peel and chop the apples. Cook onions and cabbage in large pot in bacon fat until browned. Add apples, vinegar, red wine, sugar, salt, cloves, and bay leaf. Cover and simmer on low heat for 2 hours. Drink a glass of the open wine bottle – don't want to waste it.

Veggie Benedict with Grandpa Jim's Hollandaise Sauce

Dave and Doug made this for us the weekend we all met in Portland. (Grandpa Jim is Dave's dad). Serves 4

- 1 English muffin for each person
- 3 egg whites (save yokes for sauce)

- 1 onion, chopped
- 4 mushrooms, sliced
- 3 kale leaves—stems removed, cut in strips
- 1 can of black beans, drained
- 1 red pepper, seeds removed and chopped
- Salt and pepper to taste

To make the veggie stir fry: fry the onion in a pan until golden brown. Put the mushrooms in pan with onions and stir them for a few minutes. Add kale, black beans and red pepper and season to taste. Put to the side.

Fry up the egg whites and put English muffins into the toaster.

Jim Monnie's Hollandaise Sauce

- 3 egg yolks
- 2 Tbsp lemon juice
- Dash of salt
- Dash of cayenne
- A couple of drops of tabasco sauce
- 4 Tbsp of butter

For the hollandaise sauce: blend all ingredients except butter, in a blender. The butter has to be melted separately and then added to the blender.

To serve: Put two toasted English muffin halves open face on a plate and top with the stir-fried veggies. Place part of the fried egg white on top and drizzle Hollandaise over the veggies and eggs. Enjoy!

Dave's Famous Hash Browns

Everyone who comes to visit our house to this day wants Dave to make hash browns for breakfast. Simple recipe, but Dave makes them taste delicious. Serves 4

- 3 Medium unpeeled potatoes (he likes to mix, red, white and purple together), shredded
- Salt & Pepper
- Cumin seeds

Heat pan on high. Grate potatoes with love and put them in piles onto the hot pan. Salt and pepper one side and turn the hash brown when one side is browned. Salt and pepper again as well and add the cumin seeds. Turn heat down to medium.

Serve with fried eggs and bacon or veggie bacon.

Mari's Family Recipes

Split Pea Vegetable Soup

I love split pea soup. When my daughter was born in 1998, Silke flew to New Mexico from Portland just before her birth. She was present in the hospital when Shannon was born. Silke stayed for three days after her birth. She took good care of Doug, me and our new baby, preparing lots of delicious, nutritious food. She also prepared some food for us to heat up once she had gone home. This split pea soup was one of the soups she prepared—she adds garbanzo beans and tomatoes, which makes it heartier and more colorful.

Makes 3½ Quarts of soup or 7 large servings

Time: 20 minutes hands-on, 7½ hours in crockpot

Place first 7 ingredients in crockpot on high, in the morning:

- 3 cups dry green split peas (a little more than 1 lb.)
- 8 cups water
- 2 tsp salt
- 1 large yellow onion, chopped
- 2 cloves crushed garlic (1 tsp jarred crushed garlic is fine)
- 2 stalks celery, chopped
- 4 large carrots, peeled and chopped

Cook in crockpot on high for 7 hours.

Continued…

To finish soup, during the last 30 minutes, add:

- 1 can garbanzo beans, rinsed and drained
- 3 Tbsp balsamic vinegar
- 1 large or 2 medium tomatoes, cored and chopped (or 1 can, diced)
- 2 tsp dried rosemary
- 2 tsp dried basil
- Lots of freshly ground pepper

Place the lid back on the crockpot and continue to heat for 30 minutes before serving to soften tomatoes and blend the flavors. Taste and season with salt, if needed.

Grandma Ony's Chicken 'n Dumplings

Silke and Mari both remember eating similar versions of chicken soup with dumplings, growing up. Mari remembers her Grandma Ony in the large farm kitchen dropping the dumplings into the boiling broth and the fragrant aroma filling the house.

The Chicken Soup:

- One whole chicken
- 1 medium onion, peeled and chopped
- 3 stalks celery, chopped
- Salt and pepper, to taste

The dumplings:

- 1½ cups flour

- ½ tsp Salt
- 1 cup boiling water
- 2 eggs

Place the whole chicken in a large stockpot with 6 quarts water and the onion, celery and seasonings. Bring to a boil. Simmer until chicken is tender and falling off the bones, approximately 1½ to 2 hours. Remove chicken from broth. Reserve broth. Cool chicken. Then prepare dumplings.

To prepare dumplings, Combine flour and salt in a medium mixing bowl. Add boiling water and mix until mixture leaves the sides of the bowl. Cool slightly. Add eggs, one at a time, beating thoroughly. Mixture will be lumpy. Return broth to a boil. Drop dough mixture by tablespoonfuls into boiling broth. Cook uncovered 15 to 20 minutes. Meanwhile, remove chicken from bones. Return chicken pieces to broth. Heat until chicken is hot. Serves 6.

Plum Kuchen

Plum kuchen is a popular dessert in Germany, served in many bakeries. Silke's mom made plum kuchen for me the first time I visited their village in Staig. This recipe is from my fellow R-41 friend, Kris McLenahan—an excellent cook and lover of home-cooked food.

Crust:

- 1½ cups flour
- ¼ cup sugar
- ¼ cup butter
- 2 tsp baking powder
- dash salt

Continued..

Then later add:

- 1 egg
- ¾ cup milk

Plums:

- 20-25 small Italian plums, remove pits and cut into quarters

Topping:

- ¾ cup sugar
- 2 tsp cinnamon
- 1 Tbsp flour

Preheat oven to 350 degrees.

Combine flour, sugar, baking powder, salt in mixing bowl. Cut in the butter with a pastry knife, until it is pea-sized crumbs. Then beat the egg in a small bowl and add milk. Pour liquid over dry flour mixture. Mix. Pour into greased 9x13 pan and smooth it evenly throughout the pan. Then cover wall to wall with the quartered plums, overlapping as needed. Combine sugar, cinnamon and 1 Tbsp flour in a small bowl. Sprinkle evenly over plums. Bake at 350 degrees for 30-35 minutes.

McMenamins Pub Black Bean Dip

The black bean dip was a favorite thing to order at McMenamins brew pub in Portland, Oregon, down the street from the apartment on Flanders. I was so excited to find the recipe published in *The Oregonian* newspaper one day, so I could create it at home.

Ingredients:

- 1 cup dried black beans
- 1 tsp sesame oil
- 1 tsp soy sauce
- 1 clove garlic, minced
- ½ tsp dried red pepper flakes
- ¼ tsp black pepper
- ½ tsp salt
- ½ tsp sugar
- ¼ tsp ground cumin
- ¼ tsp ground ginger
- ½ cup onion, finely diced

Serve with:

- 2 Tbsp salsa
- 2 Tbsp sour cream
- Tortilla chips

Sort and wash the beans and soak overnight in cold water to cover. Drain off soaking water and cover with fresh water in a medium saucepan (or slow cooker works well). Add oil, soy sauce, garlic and onion. Bring to a boil, reduce heat and simmer until beans are tender, 1½—2 hours, stirring occasionally. Add more water if necessary to keep beans from drying out. When beans are tender, remove from heat. To serve, top with dollop of sour cream and salsa. Serve with tortilla chips.

Delicious Chicken Parmesan

Doug made Chicken Parmesan for me for our first date in the kitchen of his dorm the year we met.

Makes 4 Servings

Ingredients:

- 4 boneless, skinless chicken breasts (about 1½ pounds)
- 1 cup all-purpose flour
- 1 cup dried breadcrumbs
- ¾ cup grated parmesan cheese, divided
- 2 large eggs
- 2 Tbsp milk
- ¼ cup olive oil, plus more as needed
- 4 cups marinara sauce (1½ jars of good quality sauce)
- 1 Tbsp dried basil
- 4 slices provolone cheese
- Salt and fresh ground black pepper
- 8 oz. spaghetti noodles

Directions:

Preheat oven to 350 degrees.

Place each chicken breast on a cutting board with plastic wrap on top of it. If very thick, cut in half horizontally first. Using a meat mallet, gently pound each until it is about ½-inch thick. Season both sides of each chicken breast with salt and pepper.

Warm the marinara sauce in a medium pan on the stove or in a microwave-safe bowl in the microwave. Set aside.

Prepare three shallow bowls with the necessary ingredients to dip each chicken breast. Bowl one contains flour and ½ tsp salt. Bowl two contains eggs, beaten, plus the milk. Bowl three contains bread-crumbs, half of the parmesan cheese, pinch of salt and generous amount of black pepper.

To prepare each chicken breast, place it in the first bowl and coat both sides with the flour. Then using tongs or your fingers, move it to the egg mixture and dip it in to cover on both sides. Finally, move it to the bowl of bread crumbs, pressing it lightly to coat on both sides with bread crumbs and place each finished chicken breast on a baking sheet.

Heat a large skillet on medium heat. Add oil to the pan to coat the bottom of the pan. Meanwhile, heat a large pot of water on the stove for the spaghetti pasta.

When skillet is hot, lay the chicken breasts in the skillet and brown them 3 to 4 minutes on each side. If your pan is not large enough for all the chicken breasts at once, work in batches until all chicken breasts are lightly browned. Remove chicken breasts from skillet and place on a bed of paper towels on a plate.

Pour warm marinara sauce in the bottom of a 9x13 baking dish, using most of the sauce, but save about ½ cup.

Arrange the browned chicken breasts on top of the marinara.

Place a large spoonful (about 2 Tbsp) of marinara sauce on top of each chicken breast. Sprinkle dried basil evenly on top of sauce. Sprinkle on remaining grated parmesan, then top with a slice of provolone cheese.

Bake, uncovered, for 15-20 minutes until cheese is melted and starting to brown.

Continued..

Meanwhile, place spaghetti in pot of boiling water and cook according to package directions until pasta is al dente. Drain pasta.

To serve, place ¼ of cooked spaghetti noodles on each plate. Using large spoon, scoop up one chicken breast with generous amount of marinara sauce and place on top of pasta noodles. Sprinkle with additional grated parmesan, if desired.

Red Sangria Recipe, Spanish-Style

Doug and I drank this by the pitcher in Majorca, Spain on the vacation that sparked our romance. Many recipes include seltzer or club soda, but the sangria in Majorca was not served sparkling.

- 1 orange, sliced
- 1 apple, cored and chunked into bite-size pieces
- 1 cup orange juice
- ¼ cup cane sugar
- ½ cup brandy
- 1 bottle Spanish red wine (like Tempranillo or Rioja wine)
- Ice (for chilling)

In a large pitcher, place fruit in bottom. Pour in the wine. Add all other ingredients and stir gently until sugar dissolves. Add ice to the pitcher and serve once sangria is sufficiently cool. Or pour unchilled sangria over ice in each glass. Make sure you get a few pieces of cut fruit in each glass. Enjoy!

Apple Dumplings (adapted from Doug's Grandma Kleiber)

Makes 6 large dumplings

Apple dumplings are a favorite fall dish at Mari and Doug's house. Both of them grew up eating homemade apple desserts of every kind each fall. They have many memories of their grandmothers making apple desserts. These dumplings are so big and delicious that we usually do not plan on making any dinner the day we make these—one apple dumpling each is more than enough for dinner. And leftover apple dumplings are allowed for breakfast the next morning in our house, too.

Dough:

- 2½ cups flour
- 2 tsp Baking powder
- ½ tsp Salt
- ½ cup milk
- ¾ cup butter

Apples:

6 large baking apples such as Fuji, Jonagold or Macintosh, peel and cut into quarters or sixths, remove cores, keeping the pieces of each apple together

Sauce:

- 2 cups water
- ¾ cup sugar
- ¼ tsp cinnamon
- ¼ tsp nutmeg
- ¼ cup butter

Preheat oven to 375 degrees.

Combine dough ingredients except butter. Then cut the butter in with a pastry knife. Add the milk last. Hand form to make a long log. Set aside.

Prepare the apples, keeping the pieces of each apple together.

Bring the sauce ingredients to boil in a small saucepan. Simmer until sugar is dissolved. Set aside.

Divide dough in half. Then divide each half into 3 equal portions to get dough balls that are each ⅙ of the dough. Working on plastic wrap for each dumpling, use plenty of flour so the dough is not sticky and roll out ⅙ chunk of dough. Lay the pieces of one apple, sprinkle of cinnamon and pat of butter on the dough. Form the apple chunks back into an apple shape as much as you can. Wrap the dough around the apple chunks and press the edges of dough together to form a dumpling. Place the dumplings in 9x13 baking pan with the pressed-together part face down in the pan. Repeat with remaining 5 apples and dough chunks.

Once all 6 apples dumplings are placed in the baking dish, carefully pour over the sauce mixture in between the dumplings (not on top of dumplings).

Place baking dish in the oven and bake for 35-45 minutes until golden brown. Serve warm or room temperature with ½ and ½.

Wacky Cake (Vegan Chocolate Cake)

The cake is a classic, moist chocolate cake that my mom made for birthdays when I was growing up. It holds together well if you need to cut it into a shaped cake, such as Raggedy Ann. It is the birthday cake of choice for my kids today. They like it as a double layer cake with cherry pie filling in between layers and Cool Whip topping on top.

Preheat oven to 350 degrees.

Stir together in large mixing bowl:

- 1½ cup flour
- 1 cup sugar
- 3 Tbsp cocoa powder
- ½ tsp salt
- 1 tsp baking soda

Then pour in:

- 1 Tbsp apple cider vinegar
- 1 tsp vanilla
- 5 Tbsp oil (I use mild flavored olive oil, or you can use avocado oil or vegetable oil)
- 1 cup water

Beat well. Pour into greased and floured 8-inch round pan and bake for 30-35 minutes. Also works well for cupcakes. Makes 14 cupcakes—bake for 20 minutes. If making a layer cake, double the recipe to make 2 8-inch round cakes.

Olga Sandwiches

Named after my mom's first boss, these baked "sandwiches," served warm, were my brother's and my favorite dinner when we were young. A good comfort food.

Ingredients:

- 8 slices white bread
- ½ pound ground beef
- ¼ cup onion, chopped
- 2 Tbsp celery, chopped
- 1 Tbsp yellow mustard
- ½ tsp salt
- 1 cup cheddar cheese, shredded or 4 slices cheddar

- 1 egg, beaten
- ¾ cup milk
- ½ tsp salt
- ¼ tsp dry mustard

Directions:

Preheat oven to 350 degrees.

Toast bread and butter each slice on one side. Brown ground beef in medium skillet. Add onion, and celery and sauté 10 minutes. Stir in yellow mustard and salt. Remove from heat. Combine next four ingredients in separate bowl. Place 4 slices of buttered toast face down in a 9x9 baking dish. Divide meat mixture evenly on bread slices. Top with cheese and place remaining four slices of toast on top. Pour egg/milk mixture over the top of all sandwiches. Bake for 30-35 minutes until golden brown.

Photos

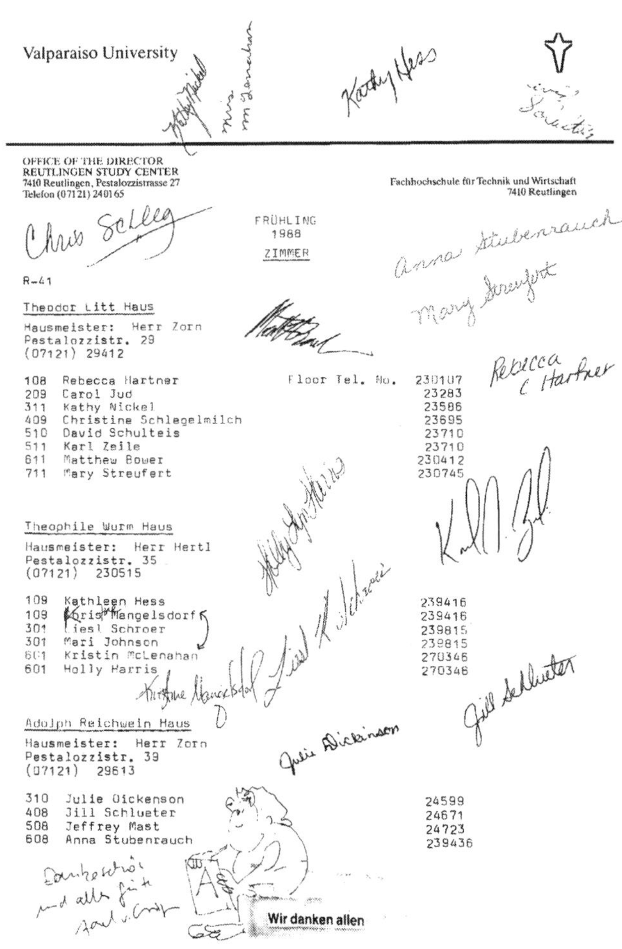

Valparaiso University

OFFICE OF THE DIRECTOR
REUTLINGEN STUDY CENTER
7410 Reutlingen, Pestalozzistrasse 27
Telefon (07121) 2401 65

Fachhochschule für Technik und Wirtschaft
7410 Reutlingen

FRÜHLING
1988
ZIMMER

R-41

Theodor Litt Haus

Hausmeister: Herr Zorn
Pestalozzistr. 29
(07121) 29412

		Floor Tel. No.
108	Rebecca Hartner	230107
209	Carol Jud	23283
311	Kathy Nickel	23586
409	Christine Schlegelmilch	23695
510	David Schulteis	23710
511	Karl Zeile	23710
611	Matthew Bower	230412
711	Mary Streufert	230745

Theophile Wurm Haus

Hausmeister: Herr Hertl
Pestalozzistr. 35
(07121) 230515

109	Kathleen Hess	239416
109	Kris Mangelsdorf	239416
301	Liesl Schroer	239815
301	Mari Johnson	239815
601	Kristin McLenahan	270346
601	Holly Harris	270346

Adolph Reichwein Haus

Hausmeister: Herr Zorn
Pestalozzistr. 39
(07121) 29613

310	Julie Dickenson	24599
408	Jill Schlueter	24671
508	Jeffrey Mast	24723
608	Anna Stubenrauch	239436

Wir danken allen

This is the roster for R-41—the Spring, 1988 Valparaiso University group to go to Reutlingen, Germany. One our last day we all signed it, including our teachers, the way you might sign a yearbook, as a souvenir.

Mari's special occasion journal spanning time from 1979 to 1988.

Mari and Silke 1991 in the Portland apartment on Flanders

Above on left: Silke's parents in Fall, 1990. Above on right: Taken in front of Mari's parents' house in 1990, Billy C. Merchant dressed as a cowboy, Mari and Silke wearing watermelon dresses made by Liz Kram. Bottom photo left to right: Doug, Mari, Silke, and Dave in 1993 in Kansas City the weekend of Mari and Doug's wedding.

Dave and Silke in 1991

I feel so close to you. But we haven't known each other very long. Two and half days, then a week and a half apart. Then six days together. That's ju eight and a half days together, plus a few weeks occasionally talking on the phone. Is that long enough to decide to move to the other side of the world

YE

Eight and a half days. What does that number mean? There are people I have known for years, but I barely know them. And I will probably always barely know them. So what if it were eight and a half years. What does <u>that</u> number mean?

But in just one day, I knew more about you than I will ever know of those people. I knew you were a sincere, caring person. I knew you were a person who trusts. In a foreign land among new people that spoke a different language, you trusted me to lead you into new experiences, adventures, and situations where you had no idea what would happen next. You followed, unflinching. (In four months, YOU will be the leader!) I knew you were a person that thinks about right and wrong, and has an open mind to new ideas. I knew we shared many common thoughts about the world and people. I knew I enjoyed your company, and I knew you enjoyed mine.

And what did time have to do with that? Time does not have the same effect two relationships. We have discovered much about each other in eight and a half days. More time will strengthen what we have found, and delight us wit more discoveries to come.

Above: Envelope of a letter from Silke to Dave,
Below: Part of a letter from Dave to Silke in the fall of 1990

Silke and Mari, June 2018, being goofy after a whole day of editing Crossing Boundaries at the Writers Retreat, a.k.a. Alice and Bob Johnson's house.

Mari (left) and Silke (foreground), June 2018, hard at work, scouring family recipe books and old letters and journals to put the finishing touches on Crossing Boundaries.

left to right: Dave, Silke, Mari and Doug in February, 2018 on a trip to San Luis Obispo, California to drink wine and enjoy amazing restaurants on the Central Coast.

Epilogue

30 Years Later.......

Mari and Doug:

We live in Valparaiso, Indiana, coming around full circle from where we met. We live just a few miles down the road from Valparaiso University. We have two kids - Shannon is in college and Kyle is in high school. Two adoring Labradoodles also share our lives. I, Mari, am a health coach and massage therapist. My first book, Gut Guide 101: Three Weeks to Better Digestion and Increased Energy is available on Amazon. We still love to travel and have recently returned from a family trip to Germany and Denmark. Another recent trip found us exploring British Columbia, Canada with its majestic mountains and endless scenic beauty.

Silke and Dave:

We still live in Portland, Oregon where we raised our daughter, Lucca, with 2 cats, 3 chickens and anywhere from 2 to 15 bunnies at any given time. None of the animals were harmed or eaten for a Sunday feast. Modern technology makes it easy to stay closely connected to my friends and family in Germany. We still love adventure and traveling with our camper van, mountain bikes and kayaks in the back. North America here we come.

Started a business together:

In 2003, Silke and Mari decided to become business partners in the apartment rental business in Portland, OR. Silke had taken classes in property management and had started her own property management business. Mari had long been interested in real estate and they decided to purchase an apartment building with Silke's company providing the property management. The venture was a success and eventually Dave and Doug got involved in the business as well. As you can imagine, there is never a dull moment when managing tenants and apartment buildings. All of the stories the four of them could tell would fill a whole book on its own! The four of them continue to be great friends. They love to get together a couple of times each year to cook, eat, drink and enjoy life.

Mari: Even now, when I open the jar of *Herbes de Provence* in my spice cupboard, it takes me right back to the dorm kitchen in Reutlingen—standing next to Silke at the stove, remembering my time there back in 1988.

Silke: We cook *Käsespätzle* together every time we get together—it is the signature dish of our friendship.

Mari: And Silke's *Käsespätzle* is still one of my favorite foods on the planet.

Silke: Aaawww. I love you, Mari!

Thank you to:

We have so many people to thank for making this book possible.

We want to thank everyone who works to make study abroad programs a reality—thank you for making the world more accessible to high school and college students everywhere. You truly change lives.

We are grateful to Mari's parents, Alice and Bob Johnson, for their help in planning our 1990 trip and most recently for providing two wonderful weeks of Writers Retreat at their home in Kansas City, complete with daily signature cocktails, gourmet meals and editing advice. This book would not have been possible without them. We could just concentrate on writing without interruptions. Thanks to Dave's mother Bonnie Scott for proofreading two of our edits.

And we are forever thankful to Mari's relatives and friends throughout the U.S. who were happy to host us in 1990 in their spare room or on a couch, especially Doug Hahn and his roommate, Dave Monnie.

Our kids, Shannon Hahn, Kyle Hahn and Lucca Monnie have been very supportive of us writing the book. They have especially helped cook, taste, and edit the recipes.

And thank you to our editor, Caroline Tolley, who helped make this book much more readable and meaningful.

Made in the USA
San Bernardino, CA
14 September 2018